African American Miners and Migrants

African American Miners and Migrants

The Eastern Kentucky Social Club

THOMAS E. WAGNER
AND PHILLIP J. OBERMILLER

❦ ❦ ❦

Afterword by William H. Turner

University of Illinois Press
Urbana and Chicago

Unless otherwise noted, the illustrations in this book are from the
collections of the Appalachian Archive, Southeast Community College,
Cumberland, Kentucky, and are used with its permission.

Library of Congress Cataloging-in-Publication Data
Wagner, Thomas E.
African American miners and migrants : the Eastern Kentucky
Social Club / Thomas E. Wagner and Phillip J. Obermiller ; afterword
by William H. Turner.
p.   cm.
Includes bibliographical references and index.
ISBN 0-252-02896-1 (cl. : acid-free paper)
ISBN 0-252-07164-6 (pbk. : acid-free paper)
1. Eastern Kentucky Social Club—Biography. 2. African Americans—
Societies, etc. 3. African Americans—Interviews. 4. African American coal
miners—Kentucky—Social life and customs. 5. Mining camps—
Kentucky—History. 6. Rural-urban migration—United States.
7. Kentucky—Social life and customs. 8. Mountain life—Kentucky.
9. Benham (Ky.)—Biography. 10. Lynch (Ky.)—Biography.
I. Obermiller, Phillip J. II. Title.
E185.5.W34   2004
305.896'0730769154—dc21   2003012089

For the members of the Eastern Kentucky Social Club—
may your friendships, joy, and spirit endure.

My Native Mountains

I love my native mountains,
　　The dear old Cumberland,
Rockribbed and everlasting,
　　How great they are, and grand!

I love each skyward reaching peak,
　　Each glassy glade and dale,
Each moss-and-fern-clad precipice
　　Each lovely flower decked vale.

I love each vine-hung rocky glen
　　I love each dark ravine
Though there may hide the catamount
　　And wild dog sly and mean.

I love my mountains' forests
　　Varied and beautiful
I love her springs and waterfalls,
　　So pure and wonderful.

I love her richly plumaged birds
　　The pheasant and the jay,
The merry scarlet tanager,
　　The woodpeck bright and gay.

How oft among these mountains
　　Has the silvery music clear
From the lark's throat cheered the traveler,
　　And the honest mountaineer.

But more than these old mountains
　　Which with wonder I revere
I love with true devotion
　　The people who live here.

So here's with love sincere and dear
  For her sons of brawn and worth;
And her daughters pure and lovely,
  The fairest types of earth.

—From Effie Waller,
  Rhymes from the Cumberland (1909)

Contents

Preface

Many years ago, we began a journey toward understanding why people in the Appalachian mountains would want to leave the region, learning more about the difficulties they faced and exploring their life experiences in their new homes. Along the way, we became especially interested in the organizations formed by these migrants that enabled them to maintain connections to their mountain heritage. We were already familiar with the migrants who came to Cincinnati, where they organized the Urban Appalachian Council and celebrated their heritage with an annual Appalachian Festival; although not from the mountains, we both had played minor roles in the creation of the council and the festival. Our academic backgrounds and natural curiosity led us to more detailed studies about urban Appalachians and their organizations. And so our journey began.

Since 1990 we have interviewed nearly a hundred individuals in Cincinnati, Dayton, Columbus, Akron, Cleveland, Hamilton, Detroit, Chicago, Baltimore, and parts of Kentucky and West Virginia. Many were founders of urban Appalachian groups or had worked very closely with migrant organizations. We have written conference papers, articles, book chapters, and books as a result of our efforts.

In our travels we came to the Eastern Kentucky Social Club (EKSC), a group of black Appalachian migrants, which began in Cleveland. With the help of William H. Turner, a member of the group, we set up interviews with several officers of the EKSC. Sitting in the homes of EKSC members in Cleveland, Detroit, Lexington, and in Benham and Lynch, Kentucky, we heard not only about "the club" but also about their fond memories of the places they had left behind in the mountains. We were intrigued by the stories of their early lives in Benham and Lynch. What was it about these communities that had instilled such strong positive memories? After all, these were coal company towns, with all the negative characteristics of such communities; many of the migrants had grown up there when the mining industry was in decline, at the end of the depression and during World War II. What was it about the Eastern Kentucky Social Club that so excited people living in cities outside the region? Why had many of these migrants devoted so much of their time to building and sustaining their organization? We set about trying to find the answers to such questions about this group of African American miners and migrants. This book is the result of our efforts.

We would like to thank each of the Eastern Kentucky Social Club members we interviewed for the warm reception we invariably received. We are especially grateful to Bill Turner, known to most EKSC members as "Billbo," who was unfailingly generous with insight, encouragement, and advice and whose Afterword brings a firsthand perspective to this book.

We are also indebted to Robert Gipe, Theresa Osborne, and Larry LaFollette at the Southeast Kentucky Community College Appalachian Archives for their assistance; to Rose Kent for reviewing the manuscript; to William Bosch, who enjoys sharing his love of Lynch; and to Judith McCulloh, Mary Giles, and Bruce Tucker for comments and guidance. Although Eastern Kentucky Social Club members were most helpful in guiding us through this project, in the end we are the ones who put pen to paper and therefore hold sole responsibility for any errors or omissions in this volume. We are also grateful for Sue Wagner's and Katie Brown's patience with innumerable "road trips" to archives, conferences, and interviews.

Throughout this narrative we have tried to keep a balance between the objective historical reasons for Eastern Kentucky Social Club members remaining so close to their Harlan County heritage and the profoundly personal reasons underlying their reverence for "these old mountains" and "love with true devotion" for the people who lived there. These are, indeed, the ties that bind them.

African American Miners and Migrants

Introduction

The life of poet Effie Waller Smith encompassed much of the history of the people described in this book—black Appalachian migrants from the eastern Kentucky coalfields. At first, it seems Effie Smith would have little in common with the members of the Eastern Kentucky Social Club, most of whom lived in coal towns and were miners or are the children of miners. There is no evidence that the poet ever lived in a company town or a coal camp, even though some of her students probably did, because major coal operators opened mines in Pike County while she was teaching there. However, her strong attachment to the mountains and to the people who lived in them, as shown in her poetry, is where she shares a deep common bond with members of the EKSC.

Effie Waller Smith was born in 1879 on Chloe Creek in the Cumberland Mountains. Her parents, farmers and former slaves, lived about four miles from Pikeville, Kentucky, the site of a thriving slave market in the early nineteenth century. The U.S. Supreme Court struck down the Civil Rights Act of 1875 when Effie was five years old, and segregationist Jim Crow laws governed race relations across eastern Kentucky by the time she was seventeen. She attended each of the eight grades available to her in the local segregated school system, moving on to the Kentucky Normal School for Colored Persons in her early twenties.

During the first years of the 1900s, Effie Waller Smith taught school and wrote poetry. She was known locally as "Miss Effie" and nationally, through the publication of her poems, as the "singing poet of the Cumberlands." It is possible that she had to keep her race hidden from her New York publishers in order to get her poems accepted. While she was still writing and teaching in Pike County, fifty miles to the south the sound of axes and saws began ringing on Looney Creek in Harlan County.[1]

In the spring of 1910, the Wisconsin Steel Company, a subsidiary of International Harvester Company, hauled the components of a sawmill thirty-six miles over mountain roads to Looney Creek, where the company intended to open a coal mine. By midsummer, workers were cutting and planing timber to construct the infrastructure needed for coal mining operations and to house workers and their families. Seven years later, the U.S. Coal and Coke Company, a subsidiary of the U.S. Steel Company, started construction of a company town farther up Looney Creek to broaden its coal mining operations. Thus began the Kentucky towns of Benham and Lynch, which would eventually attract thousands of African American miners. Other towns, such as nearby Cumberland, also played a role in this part of Appalachian history. Because it was primarily Benham and Lynch that became the "home place" of the Eastern Kentucky Social Club, they serve as our main focus in this book.[2]

At their peak, the two company towns would have a combined population of nearly ten thousand residents, with African Americans composing nearly 25 percent of the total. After World War II, many residents migrated to northern urban areas, and it was a small group of these migrants in Cleveland, Ohio, who founded the Eastern Kentucky Social Club.

The ties that bind black Appalachians to their mountain heritage are not immediately obvious. In addition to segregation, violence against blacks was a dreadful part of mountain life. At least six and possibly ten black mountaineers were lynched during the period Effie Waller Smith lived in eastern Kentucky.[3] Coal mining itself has always been a dangerous occupation, and the suffocating paternalism in many company towns would seem to allow little opportunity for black miners to develop personally, much less form a cohesive group identity. Given those circumstances, it seems most black miners and mountaineers would want to break with their past. The members of the EKSC, however, have chosen not to disown their roots in Harlan County but to celebrate them.

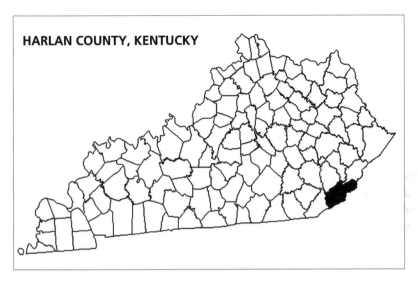

Harlan County, Kentucky. (From the *Kentucky Atlas and Gazetteer*)

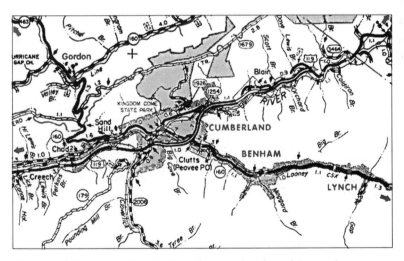

Cumberland, Benham, and Lynch. (From the *Kentucky Atlas and Gazetteer*)

Although the members of the Eastern Kentucky Social Club are the primary focus of this book, there are other, equally important, themes to consider. Among them are the unique characteristics of "model" coal towns and the role they played in the Appalachian region and the lives of their residents. Further, model coal towns have often been overlooked in the context of a contemporary national trend of welfare capitalism and building planned corporate towns. Finally, although there is a growing collection of literature about African Americans in Appalachia and about black coal miners, few of these accounts have been about black coal miners who lived in southeastern Kentucky or African Americans who migrated to northern and midwestern cities from that area.

We provide context for the Eastern Kentucky Social Club by beginning in the first three chapters with a brief overview of African American history in Appalachia, followed by an examination of black experiences in Appalachian coal camps and coal towns and ending with a short survey of black migration from the region. Chapters four and five provide more background by placing two key Harlan County coal operators within the larger story of the Progressive Era practices of town planning and welfare capitalism. We also describe the establishment of Benham and Lynch, model company towns built by International Harvester and U.S. Steel. In chapter six, EKSC members discuss Benham and Lynch, where many of them grew up. Chapter seven focuses on the club itself, using interviews to discuss its founding, local chapters, reunions, Memorial Day observances, and future. We conclude in chapter eight with a summary of why many negative assumptions are not coherent with the actual experience of the Eastern Kentucky Social Club members. The Afterword by William H. Turner offers the provocative reflections and insights of a Lynch native and longtime club member. We believe the interaction of our research, the interviews with club members, and Bill Turner's essay will help readers understand why members of the Eastern Kentucky Social Club share Effie Waller Smith's love for their mountain homes.

❦ ❦ ❦ "Coming Up on the Rough Side of the Mountain": African Americans and Coal Camps in Appalachia

The African American men and women who were recruited to work and live in the coal towns of Benham and Lynch were not the first blacks in Appalachia. African Americans have a long history in the Appalachian mountains. They accompanied the earliest French and Spanish explorers into the region as both freedmen and as slaves. William Turner believes that blacks in Appalachia were some of "America's *first* blacks—appearing almost a century before the landing at Jamestown."[1]

Slavery was practiced throughout the southern Appalachian mountains. Nearly a thousand black slaves, for instance, accompanied their Cherokee masters out of the region on the infamous Trail of Tears in 1838. By the outset of the Civil War, slaves could be found in every county of the region. Early scholars such as Carter G. Woodson acknowledged that but maintained that slavery was never as widely favored or practiced in the mountains as in the plantation South. In Woodson's view, mountaineers put a high value on personal freedom, equality, and independence, principles often reinforced by their Baptist and Presbyterian religious tenets. Politically, mountaineers favored abolition because of their opposition to the dominance of proslavery elites in state governments, the same elites that hindered development in the upland portions of Appalachian states. Moreover, slavery was not an economically viable option for most of the small farmers, manufacturers, and businesses found across the mountains.[2]

Contemporary researchers such as Wilma Dunaway, however, are much more critical of slaveholding in Appalachia. Dunaway's research shows that slavery was a common phenomenon throughout the mountain South and was generally more brutal than in other slaveholding areas. In particular, she notes higher rates of forced family breakup and child mortality in the southern mountains than in the plantation South.[3] John Inscoe, however, aptly refers to a "quiltlike character of highland racism." Most modern scholars point out the uneven nature of Appalachian racial practices. In Harlan County, Kentucky, for instance, slave ownership before the Civil War was concentrated among five families that owned 48 percent of the slaves in the county; the largest of the families owned fifty-eight. Historians also point out that racial attitudes were often paradoxical. Some Appalachian slaveholders fought to preserve the Union, lynching occurred in counties with strong abolitionist legacies, and blacks fled some highland counties whereas their populations grew substantially in others. "White highlanders' views of African Americans in theory and treatment of them in practice," Inscoe concludes, "were for the most part well within the mainstream of attitudes and behavior elsewhere in the South, a mainstream that was in itself by no means monolithic. . . . On either side of the Mason-Dixon line, nineteenth-century white America was racist, varying in degree and form of expression. The same was true of Appalachia."[4]

The oppression of blacks in the pre–Civil War South gave rise to the Underground Railroad, which, according to Woodson, ran through and had many stops in Appalachia. Again, contemporary scholarship provides an alternative view: "The whole notion of Appalachia as a center of Underground Railway activity is suspect," Inscoe maintains. "Most major treatments of the Underground Railroad make no reference to southern Appalachian locales."[5] Nevertheless, it would have been difficult for many men and women fleeing slavery to enter the northern states without crossing portions of what is now known as the central Appalachian subregion, which contains the mountainous counties of southern West Virginia, eastern Kentucky and Tennessee, and western Virginia. Passage would have required the active participation of at least some mountaineers and the passive cooperation of many others.

Racial violence rather than racial harmony was a reality of Appalachian life following the Civil War. In the Appalachian sections of Alabama, Georgia, Kentucky, North Carolina, Tennessee, Virginia, and West Virginia, 128 black lynchings occurred between 1880 and 1939. The number of "legal" lynchings in which the law was used to justify racial murder is unknown. The social changes brought about by industrialization also led to mob violence in the mountains. As Robert Stuckert observes, "The use of black workers as strikebreakers was often a bone of contention. It was in the coalfields that racial violence occurred most frequently."[6]

After Emancipation, railway construction and mine openings attracted black laborers and their families from the plantation South into the mountains. From the time of the Civil War to the turn of the century, the black population in the southern Appalachian mountains grew by 64 percent, to 274,000. The growing numbers of newly enfranchised voters in a relatively sparsely populated area affected the political makeup of the Appalachian portions of Tennessee, Kentucky, Virginia, North Carolina, and West Virginia. Black voters in the upper South, "where there was a relative lack of racial hostility between mountain whites and blacks," gave Republicans a political edge that would last into the twentieth century.[7]

By the turn of the century, industrial expansion in the Appalachian mountains and a concomitant demand for more laborers caused companies to send recruiters throughout the South, looking for workers. A 1919 Department of Labor Report noted, "The Negroes most sought after in the Birmingham [Alabama] district have been the coal miners. There has been a constant demand in the mines of Kentucky, West Virginia, Pennsylvania, and Virginia for the experienced miners here."[8] Indeed, the largest migration of blacks into the Appalachian region took place between 1900 and 1930, and these migration flows were focused on the coalfields. Joe William Trotter has documented that phenomenon: "The African-American population in the central Appalachian plateau increased by nearly 200 percent between 1900 and 1930, from less than 40,000 to over 108,000."[9]

The black workers recruited to Benham and Lynch by International Harvester and U.S. Steel, as well as other black migrants to Appalachia in this period, did not necessarily see themselves as permanent residents of the mountains, but they came with the same expectations as those who did. Often, they came seeking wage labor to help their families in the South, who were trapped in ever-declining economic spirals of tenant farming and sharecropping.[10] Black agricultural workers in the Deep South were particularly devastated by spreading infestations of the boll weevil, and they fled north to escape the economic consequences of that infestation. Trent Alexander notes, "The boll weevil loomed large in the black exodus not only because most of the black population resided in the cotton states, but also because the blacks in those areas were more likely to be laborers and sharecroppers, and thus particularly at risk."[11] In her first-person account of African American life in the Appalachian coalfields, Memphis Tennessee Garrison recalled, "The people who had security, who had good farms and things like that weren't moving out here. It was the people who were having a hard time trying to make a living who came."[12] The railroad routes out of the flat-land South into the Appalachian coalfields provided black migrants with two advantages: access to well-paying jobs and frequent opportunities to return

Removing slate in the Lynch mine.

Coal loader in the Lynch mine.

home for cultural refreshment. Indeed, many saved their wages with thoughts of returning to buy farms in the South.

Over time, however, many black farmers who came for temporary work in the mines would become skilled and settled coal miners. Rural African Americans were as aware of the economic implications of industrialization as their white counterparts, and they responded accordingly. On their movement into the Appalachian coalfields, Joe William Trotter writes, "Through their southern kin and friendship networks, black coal miners played a crucial role in organizing their own migration to the region, facilitating their own entrance into the industrial labor force and, to a substantial degree, shaping their own experiences under the onslaught of industrial capitalism."[13]

An important difference, however, distinguished rural black migrants to the coalfields from their white counterparts. Although many African Americans moving from the Deep South may have had dreams of buying land, most, as former sharecroppers, did not actually own any property. In contrast, most native whites and some foreign immigrants who came to the coal towns could lay claim to a landholding "back home." Although white Appalachian miners could see themselves as farmers who had intermittent jobs in the mines, in most cases black miners could not afford that luxury. Their home place was a social network located in a particular area of the South rather than the physical and economic reality of landholding. Their commitment to mining and coal-town life, at least initially, was driven by necessity and therefore more complete than that of white newcomers to the coalfields.

The black miners who migrated to Behnam and Lynch were not the first African Americans in Appalachia to be associated with mining. Blacks had come to the coalfields much earlier, although not of their own volition. William Turner observes, "Significantly, Virginia has the distinction of being the first state in which blacks were employed as coal miners. Near Jamestown, where black slaves first appeared, some five hundred blacks worked the mines in 1796."[14] By 1833 an estimated five thousand slaves were working in the gold mines of Burke County in the mountains of western North Carolina. According to Ronald Eller, "Blacks had worked in southern Appalachian mines from the opening of the first collieries. As early as the 1850s, slaves were mining coal in the Kanawha Valley [of West Virginia], and after the Civil War many of the black laborers who constructed the railroads found employment in the mines."[15]

Other African American miners got work experience under different but equally adverse circumstances. In the postbellum era, southern states often leased out their prisoners to private companies as laborers, and southern sheriffs wanted to keep their convict work gangs full because of the profits involved. Consequently, blacks in particular were brought up on false or flimsy charges and used as convict labor, often in mines. As Robert Stuckert reports, "Convicts, almost all of whom were black, were leased to coal companies in Appalachian Georgia, Alabama, Kentucky, and Tennessee, and to railroad companies in western North Carolina and Virginia." Blacks impressed into coalfield work gangs rightfully resented their condition and often "mutinied" against their captors. Nonetheless, many became able miners who, having served out their "time," stayed on in the Appalachian coalfields and worked as experienced miners.[16] "By 1890 in the Appalachian re-

gions of Alabama, Tennessee, Kentucky, Virginia, and West Virginia," William Turner notes, "blacks ranged from 46 percent . . . of the miners [Alabama] to 15 percent in Kentucky."[17]

At the beginning of the twentieth century, Appalachian coalfields were already home to a sizable population of black miners. Their experiences were often determined by where they lived and for whom they worked, factors that ultimately affected the quality of their lives and strength of their ties to Appalachia. To more fully understand the experience of black miners, they must be seen in the context of the environment in which they lived and worked—coal camps and, later, coal towns.

Coal Camps in Appalachia

More than twenty thousand coal camps and company towns were established in the United States during the first sixty years of the twentieth century; one in every ten was located in Kentucky. These Appalachian coal towns were by no means a homogeneous lot.[18] Crandall Shifflett describes them as complex social arrangements where the nature of life "depended on the nature of an individual operator, the life cycle of the town, the composition of its population, and other forces of change." Ronald L. Lewis concurs: "Company towns varied greatly, depending on when they were constructed and by whom."[19] Many of the earlier towns were set up by undercapitalized coal operators, leading to very poor working and living conditions.

Constructing worker housing, or even building a whole town for workers, predates the American experience. British coal-mining companies began the practice during the late seventeenth century. New England textile towns built in the 1790s are among the earliest American examples of company housing. By the 1850s numerous company-owned mill towns could be found up and down the East Coast, and several company towns for iron and steel workers were in existence in Pennsylvania and Michigan. Many company town owners saw the communities as a means to manage their workforce. In their view, employees could be influenced through control of their living environment. Lowell, Massachusetts, for instance, was established in 1820 by Francis

Cabot Lowell with this intent. Lowell believed that placing workers together in multi-unit housing in one community would build solidarity and loyalty among his employees.

An example of corporate feudalism during the early period of Appalachian coal camps occurred during the 1870s in the company mining camps of Tioga County, Pennsylvania, where the camps were operated as private fiefdoms. The companies maintained private ownership of the roads and railways leading into the county, thereby forbidding access to outside observers. Arbitrary rules were enforced in these camps by heavy fines and threats of worker dismissals and family evictions. By 1925 a federal commission investigating the coal industry found that "living conditions in central Appalachian coal towns were among the worst to be found anywhere in the nation."[20]

Although sharp distinctions are not possible, there were notable differences between coal camps and company towns. The camps tended to be older, smaller, less well organized, and not as highly capitalized as company towns. Camps were often the fiefdoms of individual owners, whereas towns were usually backed by larger corporate entities. Nevertheless, the characteristics of coal camps and company towns also overlapped. In this discussion, we use the designations interchangeably and sometimes employ "coal towns." Yet there were decidedly fewer similarities between the coal camps and the model towns that eventually appeared in the coalfields.

Were there a quality-of-life index spanning coal camps, company towns, and model coal towns, many negative images of Appalachian coalfield life would be found at the coal camp end of the spectrum. Working and living conditions appear to have improved from camps through company towns to model towns. Company towns in the Appalachian highlands seem to have been present as early as 1885; coal camps, although difficult to trace, were established earlier. By 1920, between 65 and 80 percent of the miners in southern Appalachia lived in coal camps, company towns, or model towns. "Model towns," as we call them, were an extraordinary form of company town. Fewer in number and usually later in development, they differed from coal towns in that they involved a great deal of intentional physical and social planning.[21]

As might be expected, company-developed mining communities

were most often found in those parts of Appalachia that were most difficult to access—the mountainous coalfields of southern West Virginia and southeastern Kentucky, for example. In the words of Robert F. Munn:

> The coal industry's involvement in the housing and social welfare of its labor force was the result of historical accident rather than conscious choice. The location of mines is, of course, dictated by the location of coal deposits. In many cases, especially in the Southern Appalachian coalfields, these deposits were remote from established communities. Local housing, stores, schools, and other facilities did not exist. In the period before good roads and the extensive ownership of automobiles, it was necessary for miners to live within easy walking distance of the mine. Thus, if a company wished to attract and retain miners, it had no option but to provide at least basic housing and a store.[22]

Munn's interpretation, however, may be a bit shortsighted. Given the necessity of establishing the rudiments of a town, coal operators looked to the economic and other benefits such an endeavor might bring to their bottom lines. Thus, a typical coal town in Appalachia was built with at least four prominent goals in mind: to attract and maintain an adequate workforce, to exploit the economic opportunities inherent in owning a town, to maintain close social control of the population, and to reap the public relations benefits in providing jobs and amenities for workers. After jobs, housing was the main attraction for workers, followed closely by recreational and shopping opportunities. In an early listing of building priorities, one coal company engineer placed "store and civic center" second and "recreational grounds, including ball diamond" third after the establishment of the tipple and other mine buildings.[23]

Company-developed towns, especially the model towns that would come later, were structured to be closed economic systems, carefully designed to recapture a portion of workers' wages or at the very least break even on corporate costs for providing housing and other employee amenities. Pay was recycled in the form of rents, interest on loans, profits from corporately owned stores and utilities, and fines levied for breaking company rules. Comprehensive control was exercised to maintain the town as a part of the company's profit structure as well

Benham miner by tracks and tipple.

as to maximize the company's power over its employees. Company towns were, in many places, feudal proprietorships that allowed no input on key decisions from a majority of the residents. Upon being asked whether miners preferred the segregationist arrangements in housing he had imposed, one coal baron responded, "I don't know whether they did or not. That's what I had for them."[24]

In writing about his own youth in a company town, novelist Homer Hickam Jr. says that he realized that life there involved more than houses, roads, schools, and mine facilities: "It was also a proposition. This proposition held that if a man was willing to come to Coalwood and offer his complete and utter loyalty to the company, he would receive in return a sensible paycheck, a sturdy house resistant to the weather, the services of a doctor and a dentist at little or no cost, and a preacher who could be counted on to give a reasonably uncomplicated sermon."[25]

Coal-town governance was often isolated from the oversight of democratic politics. Janet Greene points out that "the camps had no governmental structure apart from the company; they were unincorporated settlements within counties, administered for the purpose of coal mining."[26] Memphis Tennessee Garrison noted that, even in incorporated coal towns, corporate policy dominated the political realm: "[The company] rules the political world. In so many places, we knew when the United States Steel's votes came in, they elected whomever they wanted. If they didn't have it before the votes were counted, they'd have it when the count was finished if they wanted it. They didn't buy the votes, but they got them. They just got them."[27] U.S. Steel also helped to control political activities in southeastern Kentucky. The four voting precincts composing Lynch always returned a heavy Republican vote, and Harlan County was one of the party's strongholds in the state. Thus, the town was described as "a small kingdom ruled by the officials of the United States Coal and Coke."[28]

Coal company presence extended well beyond political influence in the local community. Hickam provides a lesson about two-dollar bills and the company's economic influence through the manager of Coalwood's boardinghouse for workers. "The coal companies like to pay in two-dollar bills. . . . That way all the businessmen over in Welch know where the power comes from in this county when they see old Tom Jefferson staring back at them. I heard tell there's more two-dollar bills in McDowell County than anywhere in the whole country."[29]

A coal company's paternalism is evident in a letter from C. F. Biggert, a vice president at the Wisconsin Steel Company's corporate offices, to Alexander Legge, president of the International Harvester subsidiary. Biggert describes the company's involvement in the religious, recreation, and social life of Benham's residents:

You will be interested in the attached pamphlet because it refers to the Benham Community Church. For about the last year and a half the Benham Community Church has been directed and controlled by our employees in the same way that a church would be supported in a small town, and the Company has no direct connection with it whatever. Also, it is practically self supporting with the exception of our Company furnishing the light and heat. At the time we had the Y.M.C.A. Association at Benham, they directed the Church and the Company paid most of the bills.

The Y.M.C.A. building is now operated as a Club but the Company employs a young man to look after same, and it has been more than self supporting since the Y.M.C.A. departed. Of course, the Company endeavors to keep good control throughout the management, handles all the accounting and buys all the supplies. We were very fortunate in getting a fine young man to conduct the civic affairs, you might say, that are a part of the Club affairs.

I am very much convinced that where employees have to do with affairs as mentioned above, and in which they are interested, with the Company giving counsel and direction in a quiet way, that the Community is much more satisfied. While the advancement may be slow as to betterment, it is much more lasting and results are more satisfactory in the end, especially when we know the people themselves are interested in making the right effort in their own way.

The moving picture house will be run by the Manager of the Club, who is on the Company's payroll. We have every reason to believe that future results will continue to be satisfactory in the operation of this motion picture house, and that it will also be more than self sustaining.[30]

Despite corporate dominance of company towns, residents were never completely passive subjects of this system of control. Margaret Crawford points out that, across the country, "Company towns became important sites of labor strife, dramatizing the continuing conflicts between capital and labor, ethnicity and Americanization, and discipline and democracy that marked industrializing America."[31] Appalachian coal towns were no exception. Blacks in coalfields had a particularly well-honed understanding of "both the extent of the company's power and its limits."[32] Both corporate power and its limits in central Appalachian coalfields can be drawn in high relief through a close examination of coal-town life.

CHAPTER 2

❦ ❦ ❦ "Life for Me Ain't Been No
        Crystal Stair":
        African Americans in Coal Towns

Although there is no evidence that racist and separatist practices were less prevalent in the Appalachian mountains than elsewhere, special conditions seem to have prevailed in coal towns. In the early days of the Appalachian coalfields, when labor shortages put a premium on workers, companies considered black coal miners to be valuable assets and actively sought them out to work in the mines. White labor agents spread out across the Deep South, accompanied by black associates "who were carefully selected for their eloquence and their willingness to disregard the truth."[1] Newspaper advertisements offering relatively generous salaries also lured black farmers to the Appalachian coalfields: "Black miners averaged $3.20 to $5.00, and even more, per eight-hour day, compared to a maximum of $2.50 per nine-hour day for southern industrial workers. Black southern farm laborers made even less, as little as .75 to $1.00 per day."[2]

The black miners in Benham and Lynch and other Appalachian coal towns found that salaries, housing, and health care offered by coal companies often far outstripped anything available to them in the rural South. Ronald L. Lewis notes that blacks in central Appalachia, particularly in southern West Virginia, "came closer to finding economic equality than in any other coalfield, and perhaps anywhere else, in America."[3] Johnnie Jones, a black miner, described why he moved from Red Ore, an oil camp near Holt, Alabama, to Harlan County, where he worked first at the Kitt Coal Company, then Benham, and finished his career in Lynch. "I left and came to Kentucky, to try to better my condition, oh which I did! . . . I don't believe I could have made it anywhere else. In fact, I know I couldn't at the Red Ore rates, I couldn't raise a big family. But after I came to the coalfields, I had to work hard though, but I made a good living, I ain't crying about it so far. And it's better since I retired. I think retired people are living better than they ever lived. It's the truth."[4]

These benefits, though, came at a price. Lewis observes that coal companies offered "the carrot of equal opportunity to all miners without regard to race or nationality and the stick of company police repression against those who did not accept complete subservience."[5] Both black and white miners were indeed closely monitored by company officials. Failure to report for a shift would bring an immediate home visit from the company-sponsored sheriff; complaints of illness or injury had to be verified by the company doctor; and malingering, absenteeism, and similar infractions that reduced production resulted in summary job dismissal and eviction from company housing. William Bosch was told by his sister that their family had been evicted at one time by U.S. Steel. "My dad was let go and evicted by U.S. Coal and Coke Co. because of a rumor that my family was brewing illegal whiskey. Dad moved the family to Louellen, Kentucky, to work at another coal company. A year later, after an investigation which indicated that the family was not brewing whiskey, the Company asked my dad to come back to work at Lynch."[6]

Jim Crow laws enforcing segregation prevailed in southern Appalachia during the first half of the twentieth century, and coal operators were not completely color blind. Black miners were often assigned to work very low seams of coal or areas that had excessive rock content, bad air, or a propensity for flooding. That entailed working on one's knees or bent double, often in pools of water, and spending a lot of "dead" or unpaid time ventilating the work area and cleaning out tons of waste rock. "I loaded coal here in Harlan County for 31 cents a ton back in the early days," said James Hannah, a black miner from Etowah County, Alabama. "We had a rough time back in those days. You go in the mines and have a rock fall, that rock was yours, you had to move that rock. Then what you loaded, you got paid for it, if you didn't load no coal, you didn't get paid."[7] As one coal operator put it, "The best points of the colored coal loader are that he will work in wet places and in entries where the air is bad with less complaint than the white man."[8]

Such conditions notwithstanding, black southerners were accustomed to strenuous work and came into the coalfields expecting to find jobs and earn their pay. Through persistence they acquired the skills and paid for the materials and tools required to drill, undercut, blast, and load coal at a mine face. Johnnie Jones walked nearly twenty miles from Benham to secure his first job:

> I didn't have no money, so all these fellows, old miners here . . . got me up a kit of tools and put it on my back and I walked all the way to Kitt Coal Company. When I got up there that morning the old man, the boss . . . he used to be the mayor of Harlan. He told me, he say, "Boy, you too late." I said "Well, your mantrip ain't run. I'm sittin' here." He said, "Well, I ain't hiring today." And I done walked all that way down there, with a kit of tools on my back. I just throwed em' on the hillside and sit down by 'em and I sit all day until they went into the mine and then they come back out. He see'd me still sittin' there. He come over and told me, said, "You got any place to stay up here?" I see'd old Sam Lee, I knowed old Sam Lee, and I asked him could I board with him, if I got the job. He told me yes. So [the boss] told me, said, "Come out in the morning," and I went out the next morning there. I went in that mine and load five cars of coal, . . . I didn't know nothing about no mining.[9]

Once in the mines, black miners quickly gained work skills and were essentially independent contractors—responsible for organizing their work, maintaining safety, and supervising and paying their helpers. "They'd let a Negro man take a section of the mines," Memphis Tennessee Garrison remembered. "He'd hire his own men and work it; they'd pay him for it and he'd pay his miners."[10] In the words of Alan Banks, "Coal miners enjoyed considerable autonomy from direct supervision at the workplace, practicing a highly-skilled craft occupation."[11] These skills included the safe, effective use of explosives, proper ventilation of work areas, how and where to place roof supports, and numerous safety practices.

Before automation, miners were paid by the ton, and black coal miners could generally control the size of their pay by dint of ingenuity and effort. Later, as automation and the declining coal market of the late 1920s exacerbated the effects of racism, the ability to produce more coal became a critical survival strategy among black coal loaders trying to keep their jobs. The work ethic black laborers had brought from the agricultural South was reinforced by company policies and by the way in which coal mining was organized. "Coal loading," Joe William Trotter states, "was the most common, difficult and hazardous inside [the mine] job and was thus more readily available." Yet blacks often preferred it because it paid more than other manual labor jobs and "provided the least supervision with the greatest amount of personal freedom in work hours." Because coal loaders were paid by the ton, they could increase their wages simply by increasing their output. Although average wage rates for coal loading were higher than most outside jobs, it was, like other inside work, subject to greater seasonal fluctuations and presented greater health hazards.[12]

Despite the hazards of mining—among them serious injury, chronic illness, and death—and economic penalties such as being short-weighed at the scales, black coal miners saw life and work in coal towns as opportunities for themselves and their families. To this extent, observes Crandall Shifflett, southern blacks were similar to the mountain whites who migrated to the camps "with the taste of poverty in their mouths." Shifflett adds, "But though poverty had claimed their attention, it had not claimed their spirits. They came in search of a better life, better schools, medical care, improved housing, and a living wage."[13]

Housing

Housing was a major attraction of company-owned towns, especially for black miners and their families. Janet Greene, for example, notes that more than "90 percent of the black mining population of the southern West Virginia coalfields lived in company housing."[14] The provision of company housing was a function of the isolation of the mining operation—there were few or no local alternatives. Making good housing available also gave employers a competitive edge in a tight labor market and a measure of control over their workforce. "My dad was lucky enough to get a job at Lynch mines," recalls Anlis Lee, who grew up in Lynch. "You could get housing from the company, so this is where he had got the house at, from the company."[15]

Miners did not own their homes, however, and therefore they lacked

Houses, lower end of Lynch, 1918.

a strong financial commitment to any particular location and were free
to shop for better wages and conditions among mining operations.
Worker mobility was, in fact, an important form of labor resistance
often practiced by black and white Appalachian miners: "Without local ties or interests, they [moved] with impunity, following the lure of
more favorable remuneration, of better living and working conditions,
until moving [became] a habit."[16] Layoffs and strikes also lessened the
value of permanent housing to both black and white miners. "By rent-
ing and remaining mobile the worker avoided making the employer the
only buyer of his labor as well as investing in housing with significant
risk of capital losses . . . the miners themselves sought to avoid owning housing in a one-employer setting in an uncertain industry."[17]

Black mobility was particularly high in Appalachian coalfields. Some
of this was caused by the cyclical nature of the coal industry. Among
other causes were blacks' refusal to take the hazardous, unproductive
work assignments they often received inside the mines and the capri-

cious—often racist—hiring and firing practices of mine operators themselves. Black miners frequently used their mobility to pursue safer working conditions, better pay, and more equal treatment. Memphis Tennessee Garrison experienced that firsthand in the West Virginia coalfields: "Now all of these people were on the go; they were a migratory set, those first miners, both black and white and foreigners. Wherever there was a new mine opening up and the possibility of better wages, they moved on. . . . I guess that's why the company didn't find it necessary to sell land and let the miners build; they just knew they'd be leaving and wouldn't pay for it, so they just rented houses to them."[18]

When black miners found living and working conditions they considered suitable, they made every effort to protect their work and housing tenure in that location. This was especially true for those working and living in model towns such as Benham and Lynch. But tenancy in company housing nonetheless remained a risky proposition. Typical leases of the day gave tenants two to four weeks' notice of eviction, but evictions in coal towns could be enforced within two weeks—immediately if the miner was fired.[19] Rents, however, were kept reasonable to attract workers and to avoid workers' demands for higher wages in order to pay high rents. Price Fishback concludes that in a sample of more than two hundred employers providing housing in the 1920s (sixty-four of which were coal employers): "The rents generally covered the costs of maintaining the housing and gave employers a normal rate of return on their investment (i.e., the same return they would have gotten from investing in other businesses)."[20] In Benham, International Harvester, for example, earned "a credit of $2,258.04" in 1920 on rental income of $46,680.02 against $44,421.98 in expenses. The rents covered "the doctors' office, the two lodge halls, the postoffice building, Chicago house [a hotel], and shanties."[21]

Companies constantly examined housing rental fees to remain competitive and maintain their investments. The coal operators in Harlan County generally shared information about what each was charging for housing. In his correspondence to Chicago headquarters, the Benham mine superintendent attached a letter from the Lynch superintendent, noting a "change in rents as well as coal and doctor. Mr. O'Connell also informs me that he had a talk with the Auditor of the Black Mountain

Corporation, who stated that they were charging $1.50 per room. Mr. Tway, President of the Harlan Operators' Association, informs me that they do not expect to make any changes in their rent."[22]

Coal companies were well aware that housing was not only an incentive for recruiting and retaining employees but also that keeping homes in good repair was a good business practice. In a letter to R. A. Walter, a Benham mine superintendent faced with a budget problem, the corporate office asked "whether it would be economy [sic] to suspend making necessary repairs when such repairs would mean the eliminating of a great deal of depreciation which might develop due to the neglect of such repair." The Chicago office then approved use of funds to repair homes despite the tight budget. "I do not believe there is any economy in letting everything get out of repair and run down. This is a situation we run [sic] up against a couple of years ago and we have since been trying to bring things to a reasonably good condition and I do not think it will be good business in a way to retrograde. You may therefore continue with the necessary maintenance of tenements."[23]

In hard times such as slowdowns, layoffs, and, in some cases, even during strikes, rents would be allowed to accrue and the company stores would carry the miners' purchases on credit, knowing that their labor would be needed again soon. Over the years, Johnnie Jones found ways to stay in Lynch, even during tough times. "Yeah, I was laid off about three or four times, what they call cuttin' you off, puttin' you on the panel. I'd go in these other little one-horse mines and I'd work there, till I could get back to Lynch."[24]

Utilities

One of the major attractions that distinguished some company towns, and model coal towns in particular, was the ready availability of electricity. The relatively small populations of Appalachia and the South, and great distances between dwellings in rural areas, made stringing lines and setting poles costly and at best only marginally profitable for electric utilities. Consequently, by 1932 only 10 percent of the nation's rural residents had electricity, compared to 70 percent of urban-dwellers. Mining, however, required electricity for illumination and ventilation as well the operation of motorized equipment. Excess generating capacity was often used in coal towns to provide electricity to miners' homes. "One survey," Janet Greene notes, "reported 80 percent of miners' homes in West Virginia had electricity in the 1920s, at least a decade before most rural farms in the state."[25] The glow of the electric light, generally unavailable outside of major cities, drew rural workers and their families to the coalfields. From the company's perspective, home electrification was a means of labor recruitment and retention. As one resident put it, "Life in a coal town was not always drab and gloomy, as some people may think."[26] Electricity, provided as part of the rent or sold outright, was also a means of income for the companies, as were sales of electrical appliances in company stores. In 1921, "electric lights" were 25 cents each in Benham and 30 cents each in Lynch. Most homes had one light per room.[27]

Another important incentive was the availability of clean water close to miners' homes. A fine grit from mining, sorting, transporting, and burning coal filled the air of all Appalachian coal towns. It coated not only miners and their tools but also outdoor and indoor surfaces above ground. In many coal camps, water for washing, housecleaning, cooking, and drinking had to be hauled for relatively long distances, often up steep inclines, and was frequently contaminated from sewage that leaked from outhouses. Model coal towns, however, offered washhouses for workers along with clean, running water, if not inside every home then most often no more than a few steps away from each dwelling. The water system that U.S. Steel built at Lynch was able to provide all the needs of the mining operation as well as furnish up to fifty gallons per person daily for residents. Looney Creek was not a reliable year-round water source, so the company drilled deep wells and built several reservoirs.[28]

Company Stores

The relative isolation of the mines gave rise to another aspect of coaltown life: the company store. Black and white miners were treated equally at company stores and waited on in turn on a first-come, first-served basis. Nevertheless, some companies engaged in price-gouging, monopolistic practices, issuing scrip (company money) in lieu of cash, and encouraging debt peonage. As a black miner said about the store in Benham, "If you worked for a company, you stayed in a company house, you traded at the company store, you bought whatever you needed out of their store. If you didn't trade there, you didn't stay there."[29]

Price Fishback has examined these practices and maintains they were generally not widespread. Most instances occurred in coal camps run by small operators during the era before the corporate consolidation of mining operations. "Company stores faced two types of competition. Where there were independent stores nearby, the companies were generally forced to meet their prices. The stores in isolated towns were able to charge higher prices, but the high prices partly reflected higher costs of transporting goods to the town, and the wages in the towns may have been higher."[30] Anlis Lee remembered that "in Lynch, the store was called the company's commissary and it was very much different from

Benham Old Store, replaced in 1920.

where we had lived before, in Virginia. . . . They had three stores here, one was a giant store, which consisted of selling furniture, clothing, or . . . if you wanted to order a car, through the store, you could get it. They'd get it for you."[31]

Company-issued scrip was most often used as a form of credit that gave miners access to their wages before they were actually due. "Miners were paid in cash monthly or every two weeks," Fishback reports. "Scrip was an advance on wages due the following payday, which was negotiable at full value at the company store."[32] Debt peonage occurred when a miner owed the company more than he was to receive on any given payday due to purchases at the company store; loans for high-cost durable goods (such as tools, appliances, furniture and, later, automobiles); or the transportation costs involved in moving to a coal town. "Debt peonage at the mines," Fishback comments, "was unusual. . . . The coal companies saw little reason to give miners scrip in excess of what they had earned because there was always the risk that the miner would leave without repaying the scrip or working off the debt."[33]

In taking a purely economic view of life in coal company towns Fishback misses the social realities that miners and their families dealt with on a daily basis. The expectation that they would patronize the company store was strongly reinforced as a loyalty issue that could be raised when deciding whom to keep during slow times and layoffs. Debt peonage was made possible by the existence of the scrip system, which kept some miners obligated to the company and led a number to financial ruin. Debt peonage also continued to be an issue after federal law required mine operators to pay workers in cash. Worker mobility was not a practical resolution of debt peonage, because "running off" on a debt owed the company could lead to a miner being blacklisted among operators in a local coalfield. Miner indebtedness, however, may have restrained mine owners, who often would continue to extend company store credit to those in debt so as not to lose the potential for repayment and to ensure an easily available workforce when the economy improved.

Black and white miners were not just the passive victims of abusive corporate practices in housing and at company stores. In good times, miners avoided exploitation by collective action, principally union organizing; by shopping at other stores that were nearby; and by moving to mining towns that had more advantageous housing and store policies. There is no question that abuses did occur in company commissaries, and striking miners often had to move their families to tent encampments outside the town limits. Over time, however, they learned to leverage the value of their labor and use their mobility to negotiate with coal operators. In addition to the physical and economic opportunities that attracted black miners to model company towns, there were many social amenities as well.

Social Institutions and Daily Life

Religion played a key role in the life of model company towns. Coal operators assisted in building worship places for almost every major denomination that workers espoused and provided meeting places for some local "associational" sects as well. The company would help build at least one community church that was to be used by all denominations, but this assistance came with strings attached. Mine operators not only gained some revenue from leased land but also gained leverage in church affairs. As Memphis Tennessee Garrison observed, "[The companies] really weren't advancing anything; it was a church they were buying. They would have a lot to say about what kind of preaching you had. The preacher would have to be in accord with the company's policy. There were always those who rebelled against certain things, but the church would have to go along with the company."[34]

While coal-town religious facilities saw constant use, they were segregated by race as well as religion. Moreover, miners' families were class-consciousness enough that they were wary of company-paid ministers who preached in company-sponsored sanctuaries. "They find that the church is allied with the industrial institution. The pastor is not of their choosing or way of doing. The presence of the better-dressed officials and their families make them not at home and may evoke a spirit of real hostility toward the church as an institution."[35] In short, religion was an important aspect of life in model coal towns but not always seen as an unalloyed blessing, because the religious institutions were under corporate control.

Benham Rising Star Baptist Church. The church was also used as the black school until a school building was constructed.

Coal operators also attempted to instill values in workers and their families by providing "wholesome" recreation and entertainment. The owners sought to encourage "American values" by providing recreational facilities such as theaters, YMCAs, and ball fields; supporting athletic teams and clubs; and sponsoring shows and events. In a letter to the superintendent of the Benham mine, an International Harvester executive expressed concern that a carnival company being brought in for the company-sponsored July Fourth celebration might not be "high class entertainment." In this and other correspondence the executive emphasized the need to entertain the people of Benham "in a good American Way on this day":

> Now, Mr. Dunbar I think it is up to you to make this a Grand and Glorious Fourth of July, and endeavor to have the people of Benham realize that it is every one's especial duty to be patriotic this year and they all should fittingly observe the Nation's birthday which means so much to all liberty loving persons. . . . I think it would be nice to decorate the Commissary, Post Office, Y.M.C.A.'s [sic] and such other buildings as you may deem appropriate and urge that a generous display of flags be made. Such a celebration should be a benefit in serving to keep the men away from liquor, but don't forget the Mothers and Children. I know it will require considerable work to carry this through, but I also know that you are the man who can do it, and I wish you all sorts of success in the undertaking. You understand, of course, that if the expenditures to make this celebration possible should exceed the specified amount it can be taken up in costs.[36]

Residents of Benham and Lynch did not rely completely on the company for recreation and fun. "We made our own recreation," said Anlis Lee. "We'd all get together on Sundays and ride [the train] from Lynch to Cumberland. . . . Also, we would just go out walking, or spend the day in the woods or mountains. . . . They did have a lot of plays at school for the kids, . . . and we'd go from house to house and listen at music. There was only record players or the radio. It wasn't television at that time. We could see as much from the radio in our minds, that children see from a television."[37] Woolford Griffey entertained himself in Benham by playing baseball. "When I was growing up I was always playing ball," he said. "They used to play ball over there by the coke oven yards, . . . everybody or almost everybody would be sittin' over there on the railroad tracks watching the game go on or either be playing. Kids, ol' folks and all."[38]

Education was also an important aspect of life in model company towns, if only because the schools served children of coal company officials as well as those of miners. Schools offered a full curriculum, including foreign languages, industrial arts, and home economics. Although legislation required segregated black and white schools, the corporate owners of model coal towns built and equipped quality structures for black students and recruited first-rate teachers from black colleges across the country. As James Laing noted about coal-town schools in 1936, "A heightened racial self-respect is given the children of Negro miners by race-conscious teachers."[39] A Harlan County newspaper gave a glowing account of the kind of schools to be found in one model coal town: "The Benham School is the pride of Educators of Eastern Kentucky . . . it lacks nothing to make it a perfect physical plant to serve its purpose. An equally well-equipped and [built] school for the colored is also provided, with home economics, manual training, play rooms and outside play equipment, which is surpassed by no school in the state for the colored."[40]

Schools gave children in model towns not only a high-quality aca-

A home economics class in Benham.

demic experience but also practice in mandatory attendance and good behavior. Several EKSC members recall that neither the company nor the families tolerated truancy or delinquency. Della Watts was unaware that children would cut school until she migrated to Cleveland, Ohio. "There was no such thing as a dropout, no such thing as cutting school either," she said about her school years in Harlan County coal towns. "I never knew kids cut school until I came to Cleveland." Gean Austin's memory is similar to Watts's. "There wasn't anything like missing school. There was no excuse. They had truant officers, if you were not here they went out to see what was wrong." A miner could lose his job and be evicted from his home if the company security identified his children as "problems." "It was an upbringing that you just couldn't imagine," Eddie McDonald says about his youth in Benham. "No kid got into any trouble because, and there is always a time when a person can get into trouble, but he was somewhat reluctant to get into trouble. All of the

Lynch Colored Elementary students, 1920.

Lynch Graded Colored School, grades 1–4, 1920.

eyes of the community, it was so small that they didn't want that family to be embarrassed or anything of that nature." An individual child's misbehavior could have serious negative consequences for the whole family and was quickly and unequivocally dealt with. "When I was coming up, you were told to do certain things, and you were not to do certain things," said Sadie Long about growing up in Lynch. "Those things you were told to do, you had to go do them. Those things you were told not to do, you better not do them, if you didn't want to get tore up. . . . A neighbor might whip you and when you went home and they told, then you'd get another whipping." Children who grew up in these circumstances not only had the benefit of good schools and well-trained teachers but also quickly learned about responsibilities to family and community.[41]

Similar conditions prevailed in the area of domestic relations in that family solidarity was reinforced, however arbitrarily, by the living conditions typical in model coal towns. Although separations and divorces did occur, they were cumbersome and costly affairs. A marital breakup guaranteed the loss of company housing, after which the miner would be assigned to a dormitory for unmarried men. Divorced women and their children lost access to the company store, housing, and schools. Moreover, they frequently had to leave their relatively secure lives in the coal towns to join relatives who lived in precarious economic circumstances. Coal company rules affecting family life came as much from concern for economic benefit as from any philosophy regarding the welfare of miners' families. As Sally Ward Maggard observes, "A family settlement pattern in the coal camps served to 'discipline' miners, provide unpaid domestic service to support the mine labor force, and increase profits for owners and stockholders. . . . The presence of wives and children acted as a stabilizing force, discouraging absenteeism and high employee turnover."[42]

Mine operators viewed common-law marriages and the cohabitation of unmarried couples in the same light as they did gambling or drinking. These behaviors were not only immoral but also not in the best economic interests of a company. Because domestic unrest interfered with production, it was simply not tolerated. Memphis Tennessee Garrison described how U.S. Steel enforced a domestic relations policy among black miners: "[The company] would send people around to see. They would ask. . . . 'You married? . . . You got your certificate?' . . . those who weren't married and weren't convincing would have to clear out within the end of the month unless they married. So, the company had a nice marriage bureau. Many of the companies wouldn't let them stay otherwise."[43]

The experiences of black women in coal towns were similar to those of their white counterparts. Janet Greene points out that coal-town women cooked for miners, cleaned their work clothes, and cared for them when they were injured on the job. In addition, most tended to gardens and livestock and produced many commodities at home to supplement the wages paid to their husbands by the coal operators. Greene notes that although "coal camps were indeed places under the complete control of company officials . . . women and their families were not passive victims of exploitation."[44]

A fortunate few such as Dorothy Morrow, who graduated from the Benham Colored School, found work in local hospitals, schools, and company stores. After graduating from Tuskegee Institute, she returned to eastern Kentucky, because, she said, "I had a desire to come back to the mountains 'cause as far as I knew, at that time, there were no black nurses working in Eastern Kentucky as registered nurses, and the second reason is 'cause I was a mountain girl."[45] Women found other jobs as well. "As domestic servants and seamstresses," Maggard notes, "some women provided goods and services for middle and upper income residents of coal towns."[46] According to a study conducted in West Virginia in 1920, women who married black miners had a rate of wage-earning, domestic-service employment almost double that of native-born white women. Joe William Trotter succinctly summarizes the political ecomony of gender among black mining families: "When it came to defining gender roles, working-class black men endorsed the home as woman's proper and special sphere. . . . Nonetheless . . . black men and women pooled their resources in the interest of group survival and development."[47]

Black children also worked in the Appalachian coalfields. "It seems to me," Memphis Tennessee Garrison recalled, "that little boys got a dollar and a quarter a day or whatever it was. I don't remember any little white boys being hired in the mines. I remember the little colored boys. Negroes were drivers of the mules that pulled the cars, and the stable bosses for a long time were Negroes. They took care of those mules. Most of the drivers were Negroes."[48] A poster announcing the 1927 July Fourth celebration in Benham provides the schedule of athletic contests for boys by age group and titles of movies that were "free to all." These celebrations were indeed subsidized by the coal operator and thus "free to all," but the theater had segregated seating; moreover, the schedule of events for white contestants was different than the "program for colored."[49] Although not unusual in itself for its time and place in American history, this example highlights the ambiguity of simultaneous inclusion and exclusion black miners and their families experienced, even in model coal towns. But African Americans in coal towns were not just passive subjects of paternalistic control and racism. They took active steps to resist and overcome those demeaning conditions.

❦ ❦ ❦ "I Don't Know Where To, but We're Moving": African American Survival Strategies in Coal Towns

In his study of southern West Virginia coal miners, David Corbin argues that the constrained atmosphere created and maintained in company-controlled coal towns strongly favored class consciousness over racial or ethnic consciousness. He maintains that the extensive corporate control experienced by residents of these towns led to antagonism between management and employees rather than interracial animosities. There were no race riots in company towns, for example, but the historical record is replete with coalfield "battles," "wars," and "massacres" stemming from company resistance to worker organizing. Corbin contends that coal operators carefully orchestrated every detail of the miners' workplaces, housing, schools, and churches to ensure racial and ethnic comity in order to keep coal production at a maximum.[1]

Some aspects of Corbin's assertion are accurate. As we will see, however, he cedes too much power to the coal operators. Social interaction in the towns was too complex to allow companies complete control over all aspects of daily life. Black and white miners and their families expressed independence not only in forming union locals but also in many other aspects of life, including attitudes toward racial and cultural differences.

Brian Kelly offers a different perspective on relations between black and white miners in coal towns. Based on his study of the Alabama coalfields, Kelly theorizes that many coal operators saw black laborers as an advantageous way of keeping down wages and other production costs as well as a key factor in preventing union organizing. Furthermore, Kelly notes, coal operators sought to maintain a mix of black and white miners in order to perpetuate racial tension. Operators exploited the bigotry of white miners by claiming that democratic tendencies of unions threatened the racial balance in the work force. Coal companies also supported middle-class blacks who encouraged black miners to resist unionism so they would not strain their relationships with generous employers.[2] As an example, George A. Ranney, secretary and treasurer of the Wisconsin Steel Company (International Harvester) wrote to the Benham mine superintendent about his "long and rather interesting talk with a colored preacher, . . . whose home is here in Chicago, but from what he told me it seems that a big part of his time is spent down in the coal fields of Kentucky. . . . going from camp to camp, trying to show his people the advantages which they enjoy and keep them happy and quiet."[3]

Miners and their families were indeed aware of racial differences, but most chose not to dwell on them. Interviews of black miners in West Virginia conducted by James Laing during the 1930s led him to conclude that "race relations are relatively intimate and friendly even though whites and Negroes work in closest contact. . . . Race consciousness is present to a limited extent among miners and to a greater extent among their children, teachers, and preachers."[4] Despite this overt harmony, racist lynchings occurred frequently in the coalfields, and racial enmity was often heightened by tension created when companies recruited black workers as scab laborers during strikes.

Sports competition displaced some racial enmity. Local black and white teams often scrimmaged against each other during the week and then played in segregated leagues on weekends. In sports, the honor of an individual coal town (and its corporate owner) seems to have been a more compelling issue than the race of the players. Indeed, some black workers were recruited more for their ability on the ballfield than their skills with pick and shovel. Willie Watts's father was "sent for, to come to Kentucky because the superintendent had a baseball team and they were losing all the time and he said he would give anything to whup this one team." The superintendent told the team's manager, "You get me a man that will beat them and you tell him he'll have a job."[5] In addition to sports leagues and athletic facilities, companies made concerts, movies, dances, parades, and civic celebrations available to miners and their families but almost always on a segregated basis.

Nonetheless, race relations in Appalachian coal towns were ostensibly cordial. As Ron Eller writes of the ambiguity of race relations among miners, "The lack of major differences in housing, pay, and living conditions mitigated caste feelings and gave rise to a common consciousness of class."[6] Apart from the separate facilities required by law, companies generally treated black and white miners evenhandedly—at least so long as the value of individual miners was determined by the quantity of coal they loaded each shift. Black miners were paid at the same rate as white miners and shopped in the same company store.

Initially, some coal towns were unsegregated. Memphis Tennessee Garrison recounts, "At first, everybody in the coal camps lived where they could get a house; everybody was too poor to be hostile to one another. At first we lived together—you lived in this house, we lived in that house, the next one lived in that house. At first when the places were new, when they were starting up, that's the way they lived. I remember that because some white woman lived in the house next from us."[7] Later, as Jim Crow laws came to prevail, blacks and whites lived in standard company houses but on separate streets. When asked about segregation in Benham, Woolford Griffey replied, "Yes, blacks were in one section, principally in one section, they had a few lived over where the main office building is now, where the colored school used to be, and the other were living on the main road above the white bridge, from there up to Lynch line. . . . some decision was made by somebody to move all the blacks out of the machine shop hollow and they segregated them up here above the white bridge, and above the road that cuts between the white and black neighborhood that goes to the main office."[8]

The generally positive attitude toward coal-town life held by many black miners and their families may seem unusual in a racist atmosphere where promotions were hard to come by for blacks in mines, unions were less than attentive to their black members, and segregation was taken for granted. Several points can be made about this perceived harmony. First, general black attitudes toward life in company towns were not that different from white reactions to the rigors of life

Lynch First Baptist Church (black).

in the coalfields. Second, coal companies attempted to manipulate the degrees of both "harmony" and "discord" among miners to their own advantage in labor relations. Third, conditions in the camps created a sense of worker solidarity. Finally, the apparent comradery between black and white miners may have belied a much deeper social discord. We will now turn to each of these points in more detail.

Lynch Mt. Sinai Baptist Church Sunday schools gathered for a picnic, 1925.

Mary LaLone studied the attitudes of people who lived in the coal towns of southwestern Virginia from the 1930s to the 1950s. She does not provide a racial breakdown of her informants but makes it clear that residents took the good with the bad: "Nearly every person interviewed recognizes and acknowledges the negative as well as the positive aspects of coal camp life. While there may be some nostalgia involved, overall the responses are quite pragmatic. The interviewees recognize the negative, exploitative aspects of the company-run system, but weigh them against the positive personal experiences they had living in the coal camps."[9]

Black miners took the same practical approach to their coal-town experiences. They had access to regular, relatively well-paying work, housing, education, health care, and recreational opportunities and could obtain credit for major purchases. They were not exempt from the effects of racism but nonetheless felt better off than their forebears and many of their contemporaries outside of the towns. That narrow perspective enabled the miners to be fairly positive, if not totally objective, about their situation in the camps. Alessandro Portelli notes that in southeastern Kentucky, "Harlan County coal miners had little opportunity to assess their condition on a universal standard of citizenship or human rights, rather than against their immediate surroundings."[10]

Portelli makes another important point about the usually positive attitude that black and white miners often expressed toward coal camp experiences. The miners had a strong psychological imperative for casting their experiences in a positive light because in doing so they "protect[ed] the image of their own manhood and maintain[ed] the appearance and belief of having some degree of free choice of environment. . . . A coal miner from Lynch, for instance, described in conversation the crowded conditions in some of the company houses even in this 'model' town and the wire fence that surrounded it. . . . Clearly he felt that it would have been demeaning to his dignity if he had admitted that he had 'consented' to live under what might have been construed as humiliating circumstances (and it would have been even more offensive to suggest that he had been forced to)."[11]

Companies themselves carefully maintained "a judicious mixture" of native whites, African Americans, and foreign-born workers in the coal towns they owned. Initially, coal operators hoped to balance the three groups' perceived cultural attitudes toward work in order to sustain high levels of production. They thought that native whites were unaccustomed to the industrial routines of mining, that blacks required fewer hours of work to fulfill their basic needs, and that foreign workers put in long hours but frequently took days off for national holidays and religious festivals. In order to ensure the tranquility necessary for efficient production by such a diverse labor force, company officials imposed artificial harmony in the camps through strict enforcement policies and severe sanctions. Companies also used the same work-force heterogeneity to pit groups against each other in an effort to defeat union organizing.[12]

Despite the machinations of the mine owners, perhaps the most appreciated aspect of coal-town life among both blacks and whites was the sense of living within a close-knit community. Gathering the oral histories of miners led Crandall Shifflett to conclude that "coal operators could not prevent the rise of a mine culture, despite their monopoly of means of social control . . . miners drew upon rural traditions to develop a work culture of their own in sports, visiting, hunting and fishing, picnicking, and other leisure activities—to make a life apart from the scrutiny of operators."[13]

Coal towns were invariably small, self-contained, densely populated places where rudimentary class structures consisted of two basic groups: miners and management. Blacks and whites "neighbored" often and easily within their own communities. Social interaction was frequent, food and favors were exchanged on an almost daily basis, and emergency assistance was just a neighbor or two away. As Andrea Massey described life in Lynch, "The people here are actually really family people, I mean they actually stick together, it's a close net of people and they will go out to help you in any way, . . . if there is a death in the community whether it's black or white, they all pull together and pull that family through." Frequently, then, this neighborliness existed between the black and white communities within a town. Black and white miners, for example, often attended each other's league games to cheer for the home team. Eddie McDonald described Benham as "a small community, it was a close-knit community that everybody knew one another and it just brought on association that brings along assimilation."[14]

Mine workers constantly faced life-threatening hazards underground, and conditions of constant physical danger made racial consicousness less pronounced. Both groups took pride in the tonnage of coal they loaded together relative to other mines, other companies, and even other towns. And, in times of crisis, there was free exchange of mutual aid between blacks and whites. "In response to the intrinsic hazards of coal mining," Joe William Trotter found, "black coal miners sometimes developed close bonds with white miners, especially during crises surrounding such catastrophes as explosions. Echoing the sentiments of many, one black miner exclaimed that 'when that mine [explosion or accident] come everybody seem like they were brothers. . . . If one man got killed it throwed a gloom over the whole mine.'"[15]

Union Organizing

Union organizing introduced another level of ambiguity to coal-town race relations. Owners used black miners as strikebreakers. William Turner, who grew up in Lynch, says that "many a black miner began his sojourn in the coalfields of Appalachia helping form an industrial labor reserve. Together with a coterie of European immigrants, blacks replaced striking native white laborers." This situation often engendered the racial animosity between white and black workers that coal operators hoped would weaken union organizing efforts. When used as scab labor, black miners were called the "albatross of Appalachia." Ronald L. Lewis agrees that not only were black miners seen as scabs, "they were *black* scabs, and the white miners displayed at least as much hostility to their color as to their status as strikebreakers."[16]

The coal workers' struggles to unionize that placed "Bloody Harlan" in the national vocabulary involved many black miners. In his history of unionization in the Harlan County coalfields, John Hevener includes several accounts of black involvement, ranging from a violent shotgun attack on deputies working for the coal companies to a miner-preacher who refused to engage in blood-letting but prayed for the union's success. But the white and black miners who fought and prayed side by side could not sit at the same table for a meal. Union organizers set up integrated "feeding stations" for strikers after hunger became rampant in Harlan County during the strikes of the 1930s. "Black miners, knowing that it would invite attack by county officials as an affront to community customs, strenuously opposed the practice and insisted on taking their meager allotment home for consumption."[17]

A sense of interracial unity emerged in the wake of successful organizing efforts that included both white and black miners. Five black delegates helped found the United Mine Workers of America in 1890, and within ten years some twenty thousand black miners constituted about 20 percent of its membership.[18] The United Mine Workers' position on race, like so many other issues involving blacks in the Appalachian coalfields, is ambiguous. It is clear that UMWA founders knew they had to overcome the divisive forces of racial and ethnic prejudices if they were to organize black and immigrant miners. "The UMW functioned as a viable, integrated trade union," Herbert Gutman notes, "and quite possibly ranked as the most thoroughly integrated voluntary association in the United States of 1900."[19] Lynch miner Gean Austin provides perspective on that point: "Well, the union itself, there wasn't any tension amongst the people, it was the company and they hired gun thugs . . . the people, they got along well even though quite a few got killed."[20]

Ronald Lewis and other historians, however, have found ample evidence that the UMWA engaged in traditional practices of racial subordination. Apart from some union locals and subdistricts in West Virginia, early-twentieth-century coal miners lived in places and times that allowed little racial tolerance. Lewis points out that black and white miners in Alabama quickly found that "even though they achieved a remarkable interracial class solidarity, when their cause challenged the segregationist norms of society, the state would smash that cause on the anvil of racism."[21] In similar fashion, the segregated society of southeastern Kentucky held no place for an integrated union.

Union drives usually elicited repressive tactics from operators, which affected and united black and white miners: blacklisting, yellow-dog contracts, labor spies, evictions, and, especially, the use of violence by armed guards. "When the UMWA, the union, began to organize in that

area," remembers Lynch native Bill Bosch, "there were no more parades
and there was no more candy and ice cream. There was just an absolute turnaround to how or what was going on within the town . . . it
was like a young war. I can remember bullets ricocheting off of the
colored high school building, I can remember my mom running men
off of our back porch, . . . it was really a dangerous situation when
organizing was being done in that area."[22]

The dangers of mining combined with the absolute control sought
by coal operators engendered among both white and black miners a
class consciousness that often superseded racial differences. Joe William Trotter emphasizes that point: "To be sure, black coal loaders
shared a variety of debilitating working conditions with their white
counterparts. Low wages, hazardous conditions, and hard work char-
acterized the experiences of all miners regardless of ethnicity or race."
Once unions like the UMWA were established, worker solidarity was
reinforced by memories of the often-violent struggles to organize as
well as by the benefits that came from unionization. The sense of unity and mutual support had limits, however. According to Trotter,
"Working-class solidarity was a highly precarious affair. . . . White
workers and employers coalesced to a substantial, even fundamental,
degree around notions of black inferiority."[23]

Interracial cooperation often began and ended at the mine entrance.
Black and white miners would emerge side by side from the portal of
Lynch Mine 31 at the end of a shift and then part ways to enter the
washhouse by different doors to shower and change clothes in a building with a wall dividing blacks from whites. The company-operated
restaurant straddling Looney Creek just outside Portal 31 served both
black and white miners but at segregated counters. Lewis is realistic
about the racial situation: "Miners lived with the ambiguities of self-
interest generated by working together underground, and [being] separated topside by social and cultural imperatives."[24]

Although segregationist Jim Crow laws drew clear color lines that
were observed across southern Appalachia, the social standards of coal
towns—indeed, of the country—dictated that black miners and their
families remain "in their place." The protocol of racism required that
black miners and their families accept the segregationist status quo

Construction along Looney Creek.

quietly. Overt challenges to the standards of segregation and its under-lying assumptions, in either word or deed, were not acceptable to the company or to the majority community. Wilburn Hayden notes that black invisibility could be considered a practical strategy: "By being invisible blacks [were] not singled out as a significant threat to the or-der of the white domain, thus able to co-exist."[25]

Although quiet, polite, even friendly interactions between black and whites in coal towns were most often conducted on a one-to-one rather than a group basis, Jim Crow laws still established the social conditions under which all black miners and their families had to live. As Hayden observes:

> When a majority member develops a close friendship with a minority individual, the individual in the majority group may see the minority individual or friend as separate from the minority group. As one moves throughout the region, it is clear that individual blacks appear to escape unequal treatment by whites. Both blacks and whites have learned to

accept the institution of black invisibility which creates the appearance of a high level of tolerance for the individual(s). The tolerance level quickly shifts to unequal treatment when the institution is challenged.[26]

That invisibility was a carefully managed survival tactic among black miners and their families. Memphis Tennessee Garrison observed, "[The Negro] has a way of camouflaging his real feelings; he can command that for use when anybody less adaptable would be completely crushed. This was necessary to survive. He learned to survive. Then he learned to be comfortable surviving. Then he learned how to boss what he had attained with his surviving. It was an evolution for him, from nothingness, from want, from ignorance on up to where he could stand as a man."[27]

Survival Strategies

African Americans in Appalachian coal towns were not just passive participants in the prevailing race relations environment. They often used hard work to maintain their job security and control their levels of income. They loaded more coal than other workers or used their mobility as an effective tactic in improving the quality of their living and working conditions. West Virginian Nannie Woodson, married to a black miner, recalled their life in the 1920s during an interview with Janet Greene: "He used to go in the mines or if he just didn't like the work he'd come out and pack up. He could get a job most anywhere. He'd go out and get him a job and get him a house and move. One time he moved me every two or three months."[28]

Black Appalachian miners also helped form labor unions, and joined and supported them as well, to gain some control over their working conditions. They also formed alliances with black organizations emerging in the early part of the twentieth century, such as the NAACP, which promoted civil liberties for all black people. Joe William Trotter maintains that black coal miners fought racial inequality in the workplace by means of three basic strategies: "high productivity in the face of white worker competition; solidarity with white workers in the face of capitalist exploitation; and, most important, a growing alliance with black elites in the face of persistent patterns of racial discrimination."[29]

In the end, however, African American survival strategies, although effective in many respects, could not withstand larger economic and social forces sweeping the country.

Coal Towns in Decline

Over time, as coal mining became a less viable occupation due to the mechanization of the mines and the changing economics of energy sources, the relatively benign situation of blacks in the Appalachian coal towns changed dramatically. Fayetta Allen, after visiting black communities in the central Appalachian coalfields during the early 1970s, found that race relations were strained: "Black Appalachians are colonized, exploited and have few or no outlets for redress."[30]

Black miners who opted to go along with the system—"fitting in" as it was called—did well by themselves and their families. The coherent system of regulation, however patronizing, provided security reinforced by company-paid police, supervisors, teachers, doctors, storekeepers, and often preachers. These mining families perceived themselves to be much better off in coal company towns, especially the model towns, than they had been in the agricultural South from which they came. Indeed, they were. As Ronald Lewis summarizes their experience, "Blacks not only were welcomed in the mountain coalfields, they were given equal wages for equal work and as good an opportunity in the occupational hierarchy as they were likely to find anywhere in industrial America."[31] As mechanization and the economic decline of coal began the gradual dissolution of the coal-town system, however, black miners and their children became aware that the next set of opportunities lay outside the coalfields. Trotter believes that "it was the onslaught of the Great Depression that revealed in sharp relief the precarious footing of the black coal-mining proletariat."[32]

The Great Depression hit just as black migration into the coalfields peaked, dramatically changing the economics of coal and job prospects for many. Some black workers lost their jobs as mines closed; others were displaced by the increasing pressure to automate mines. Despite the unions' token protection, the racist belief prevailed that black workers, although they might be expert hand-loaders, would never be competent to operate heavy mining equipment. According to Trotter, by the late 1920s, "Employers increasingly asserted that the negro is not much good with machinery."[33] For many African American miners and their families the signs were clear. It was time to take the next step in their southern exodus.

Migration

"The coal mine was good as long as they were working, but when they are not working it is pretty rough, so they all looked for better jobs," said Gean Austin about his family. "Actually kids growing up [in Benham and Lynch], . . . usually all the kids go to school and they migrate away and get good jobs."[34] Lacking job opportunities, black youths were already migrating out of the coalfields in the late 1920s and early 1930s. World War II further loosened ties by giving black workers experience outside the region in both the military and the war industries. Migration flows grew even stronger after World War II when low demand for

Coal loader Charles Gregory and his wife, Sarah, a former Benham teacher.

coal and better job prospects in the city drove many miners, both black and white, from the central Appalachian coalfields. John Hevener, who chronicled the coal age in Harlan County, wrote poignantly of this era of decline and migration:

> Because of declining national demand for coal, soaring rail transporta-
> tion costs, and inability to match its competitors' mechanization, the
> Harlan coal industry fared poorly with rigid regulation of both freight
> rates and wages. After exceeding fifteen million tons for a second time in
> 1942, over the next two decades annual production plunged to under four
> million tons. Simultaneously, Harlan miners tripled their productivity,
> which, coupled with shrinking production, reduced the number of em-
> ployed miners from 15,864 in 1941 to 2,242 in 1961. Although the county's
> population plummeted from 75,275 in 1940 to 37,370 in 1970, the mass
> exodus to Cincinnati, Cleveland, Chicago, Dayton, and Detroit proceed-
> ed too slowly to avert widespread unemployment and poverty. In 1959,
> five thousand local miners were unemployed, 40 percent of the county's
> people were existing on union or government pensions, and more than
> a third of them were receiving surplus food rations. Because of the ar-
> ea's isolation, a reputation for labor militancy, and union resistance to
> low-wage industry, no new industries provided an alternative to mine
> employment.[35]

Layoffs due to the declining economics of coal and the refusal to train black miners to handle the new automated equipment overwhelmed the African American mining community in the mountains. Ronald Lewis provides a succinct accounting of the decreasing numbers of Appalachian coal miners: "Between 1950 and 1970, the white work force fell from 483,818 to 128,375 men, a decline of 73.5 percent. The effect on blacks was even more devastating as their total plunged from 30,042 to 3,673, a reduction of 87.8 percent in twenty years." It was equally overwhelming in human terms. William Turner remembers several mornings when he woke to find his Lynch friends and neighbors sim- ply gone, having abandoned their company homes and debt for the promise of jobs in the urban North. These were emotional times for those who left as well as those who stayed behind. Not all those who migrated, however, remained in the city. Woolford Griffey, for exam- ple, returned to Benham. "Oh yeah," he said. "I wouldn't live anywhere else. I spent five years in the city, almost five years in the city, in Pittsburgh, Pennsylvania. And I saw too much."[36]

Black miners who migrated from Benham and Lynch and other towns in Harlan County did not just disappear. For them, the cities of the Midwest held both opportunities and allure. Frustrated by frequent layoffs, mine closings, a lack of promotions, and the parochialism of coal-town life, displaced miners—black and white—saw better prospects in the metropolitan areas of the North. In the post–World War II economic expansion, northern factories were actively looking for workers. The manufacturing jobs they offered paid higher wages, were frequently less arduous, and involved less danger than coal mining. In addition, migrant families could put women and children to work in the urban labor force, greatly increasing household income—an option not as widely available in coal towns.

Black migration from the mountains took a familiar form says William Turner. "The long-standing Southern extended-family pattern was not generally interrupted in the move into Appalachia. . . . Its stability has been noted as a life-sustaining link between mountain enclaves and the urban communities of the Midwest. Though generally well adjusted and assimilated in the industrial centers and suburbs, three generations of mountain blacks have developed strong family and community-of-origin networks."[37] This extended family system meant that although there was a huge exodus of black workers and their families from Appalachian coalfields, the region remained home to many African Americans.

There is evidence that black migrants from Appalachia quickly assimilated into urban black communities in their new places of residence. Eddie McDonald, who worked forty-two years for the Chrysler Corporation in Detroit, was typical of many black Appalachians: "I never had any problems in finding a job . . . as I said, the job market was really booming at that particular time. I was working two jobs, two shifts at that particular time in the forties."[38] The socioeconomic differences found between Appalachian blacks and non-Appalachian blacks in Cincinnati, for instance, were minor. William Philliber and Phillip Obermiller report that in the city, "Black Appalachians experience the same life chances as other blacks. They are restricted by being black, but they are not further restricted because they are Appalachian. . . . Black Appalachians have become part of the larger black group."[39]

The economic assimilation that these accounts suggest cloaks the social reality of many black migrants' attachment to their mountain backgrounds. They may have been part of the urban black community, but their roots remained in the mountains. That is especially true of migrants from the coal towns of Benham and Lynch in southeastern Kentucky, where a common heritage of experience, memories, and acquaintances formed a vital social network among African American migrant families. Many of these shared experiences were shaped during the Progressive Era that began at the turn of the twentieth century. During this time American industrialists implemented two industrial policies, corporate community-building and welfare capitalism, that would have lasting effects on American labor relations and, in particular, on miners from Benham and Lynch.

❦ ❦ ❦ "Sing a Song of 'Welfare'": Corporate Communities and Welfare Capitalism in Southeastern Kentucky

Between 1900 and 1930 Harlan County, Kentucky, the setting for Benham and Lynch, underwent a rapid transformation from an agrarian, pre-capitalist economy to a heavily industrialized area owned and controlled by large corporations. Harlan County's big new industry was coal mining. The first trainload of coal was shipped out of the county in 1911, and by 1928 nine major coal seams were producing more than fourteen million tons a year.[1] Since joining the retinue of King Coal at the beginning of the twentieth century, Harlan County's population has reflected the economics of mining.

There were relatively few miners in Harlan County in the early 1900s, but their numbers rose to 7,391 in 1920 and to 11,920 in 1930. In 1930 coal miners constituted 75 percent of the county's male work force. The majority lived in Benham and Lynch. According to Alan Banks, "In 1920, just three corporations, the Wisconsin Steel Company, Black Mountain Corporation, and U.S. Coal and Coke, produced approximately 50 percent of all coal mined in Harlan County." Banks points out that the growth of large corporate owners extended their hegemony over the local coal industry by forcing out other, smaller operators: "As the number of Harlan County coal employees per firm increased from 95.5 in 1920 to more than 300 in 1930, the number of active coal companies decreased from 75 to 38."[2]

Model towns such as Benham and Lynch in the southeastern corner of Harlan County were founded by large and well-financed corporations, International Harvester and U.S. Steel, respectively. The *Har-*

lan Daily Enterprise provides a flavor of how these places were perceived, at least by a sympathetic local press: "The great pioneering of the modern world has been accomplished through the relentless urge of big Industry and fortunate is that community which is pioneered by a group of big business men who can vision not only the development of their interests but who can see farther into the future, homes, citizens, and life of its own industrial family. Such a fortunate community was Benham."[3]

Benham and Lynch were indeed models of their kind, but in fact they represented a very small fraction of company towns in the coalfields. Ron Eller points out that "such communities offered a variety of social opportunities for the miner's family and provided a stark contrast to the average mining town. Yet, they typified less than 2 percent of all the company towns in the southern Appalachian coalfields and touched the lives of only a fraction of the mining population in the mountains."[4] It is precisely these model towns, however, that are the primary source of Eastern Kentucky Social Club membership.

Corporate Communities

Although Washington, D.C., and Savannah, Georgia, are exceptions, few communities in the United States were planned and built "from scratch." Certainly, the concept of town planning is centuries old and can be seen in cities that grew from early settlements throughout the world. The structured arrangement of streets and public spaces at Knossos in Crete, Ayutuya in Thailand, or in former Roman towns and military camps is evidence of early town planning. Even so, most of today's towns or cities developed from small unplanned settlements that attracted a growing population, typically because of economic factors. Some of these communities began as transportation crossroads, others were the focus of government or commerce, and still others grew because jobs were available in a nearby mine or industry.

Despite the early experiments in Lowell, Massachusetts, and later in Pullman, Illinois, and Gary, Indiana, city planning in the United States during the early decades of the twentieth century was almost nonexistent. In 1914 there was only one full-time municipal planner in the

United States. Even so, as a result of the garden city movement in England and the city beautiful movement in the United States there were several efforts to design and build planned communities. Mariemont near Cincinnati, Palos Verde in California, and Kingsport, Tennessee, were among several attempts to construct new and modern towns. Although some planned communities were intended for working-class residents, the majority were expensive residential areas for the upper middle class.[5]

City planning was still forming as a discipline, but several planning techniques that still persist were employed in the construction of many company towns, including Benham and Lynch. Company towns were often built on a linear grid (Lynch) or curvilinear (Benham) plan. Most homes in both communities appear to be designed by architects; at least twelve distinct home designs were used in Lynch. Both towns were constructed considering the advantages and constraints of the sites, to allow for future growth, and to provide the conveniences of established cities.[6]

Lynch, July 1920.

Building Site East Center
Jan. 18, 1919.

Benham, 1919.

The development of Benham and Lynch was not so much a function of the new planning notions emerging in the United States but of necessity. The coal that International Harvester and U.S. Steel wanted to mine was located in an isolated area, and both companies had to construct communities for workers and to house support services for mining operations.

Although the towns were planned communities, they were designed by corporate engineers—not urban planners—for the purpose of facilitating coal mining. By 1910 Frederick Winslow Taylor had popularized the concept of "scientific management": the rationalization of the manufacturing process through time and motion studies, systematic accounting and purchasing procedures, and hierarchical levels of management that brought efficiency to the workplace. At the core of the scientific management movement was a professional trained to rationalize systems and propose logical solutions to problems—the engineer. Social problems were no exceptions; in fact, Taylor's philosophy served to "elevate the status of engineer to that of social reformer, and to see in scientific management a method for achieving far reaching social, political, and economic reform."[7]

In telling the story of Benham, the International Harvester Company magazine was clear that building the town was a practical business decision: "Coal, by its very nature, is usually found in inaccessible places. To enable men to mine it efficiently, living quarters near the mine must be made available. Since no accommodations for employees were in existence when the operation started years ago, Harvester was forced to build them. Along with the homes—there are more than five hundred of them now—shopping facilities, schools, roads, and all the other conveniences city dwellers take for granted had to be constructed."[8]

Beyond the obvious economic potential of the housing, stores, and physical infrastructure in model coal towns, there was another, less-well-articulated component. The towns were organized around a theory of social control, ostensibly for the betterment of workers and their families but, in fact, to protect the interests of corporate owners. Despite U.S. Steel's claim in 1906 that "the most successful attempts at industrial betterment in our country are those furthest removed from the suspicion of domination or control by the employer," the paternalism implicit in the very concept of "industrial betterment" remains clear.[9]

Maintaining tight control of the work force and local community was a key aspect of company town philosophy that was only exacerbated by later unionizing efforts. Alessandro Portelli provides an example of this when he notes that even in the model corporate community of Lynch, "company guards escorted all strangers who came in at the train station to the company office, where they were asked to justify their presence in the camp or leave. The town was surrounded by a wire fence, explicitly intended to keep the organizers out." It is no coincidence that Harlan County was the last coal county in the nation to agree to make its mines union shops.[10]

Throughout the early years of Lynch, however, the company ruled in a benevolent and humane manner, and employees were not bothered by the petty harassment found in many smaller coal towns. In fact, until union organizing became an issue, company police did not lock

International Harvester Company police in Benham.

the gate across the entrance road at night.[11] Even so, the miners and their families who lived in Lynch were under the control of the company, and the fence was an ominous symbol of employer-employee relations. Obviously meant to keep out interlopers, it also symbolized the company's determination to keep in miners.

Welfare Capitalism

The employment benefits that many American workers now take for granted originated in the well-known efforts of the American labor movement and in the legislation of the New Deal. Often overlooked, however, are the abiding effects of the turn-of-the-century industrial management philosophy of welfare capitalism. Although much of the history of welfare capitalism has been written from an urban perspective, the rural Kentucky towns of Benham and Lynch were prime examples of it in action.

The American Civil War was fought, at least in part, to determine the basic relationship between labor and capital. With the issue of slavery settled, the contest for company control versus workers' rights moved in the postbellum period to the rapidly industrializing areas of the country. The debate continued throughout the Gilded Age of the late 1800s and well past the Progressive Era of the early 1900s. The closing decades of the 1800s saw the decline of small, proprietor owned and operated companies and the rise of large national corporations—an evolution from proprietary capitalism to the predatory capitalism of the so-called Robber Barons. Employees went from being co-workers who were often on a first-name basis with their small-business employers to anonymous and expendable parts in large, impersonal corporate structures with multiple layers of management and absentee ownership. These changing conditions led to worker protests such as the National Railroad Strike of 1886, the Homestead Strike of 1892, and the Pullman Strike of 1894, to name a few. Andrea Tone notes that "between 1890 and 1900 nearly twenty-three thousand strikes affecting over eighty thousand establishments immobilized close to four million workers; 75 percent of these were union ordered."[12]

Before 1900, employers' concerns focused mainly on the rise of labor unions, but after the turn of the century their fears turned toward government intervention as well. Corporate managers, already concerned about the growing union movement, became concerned that the increasing industrial unrest would attract the attention of legislators inclined to buy labor peace at the cost of corporate profits. "The public consequences of private sector conflicts," Tone notes, "invited government management of industrial relations to an unprecedented degree." Managers of large corporations such as U.S. Steel and International Harvester, among many others, decided to substitute welfare for warfare in their industrial relations. Thus began the Progressive Era (1900–1920) and the spread of welfare capitalism.[13]

As originally defined in the early 1900s, welfare capitalism was an industrial philosophy that encouraged corporations to provide employee services and benefits beyond earned wages. International Harvester's Cyrus McCormick was among the leading proponents of welfare capitalism, or "welfare work." Although viewed by some critics as anti-unionism, most corporate leaders expressed the opinion that watching after the welfare of workers through improved nutrition and health, recreation and sports, education, and better housing created healthy and industrious employees. Such employees would be more productive and efficient, it was believed, and thus increase bottom-line profits.

Under the precepts of welfare capitalism in addition to jobs, large corporations provided housing, education, health care, recreation, and even churches and stores. In exchange, workers and their families surrendered a great deal of civic, social, and economic freedom to their employers. "Welfare work," defined in a July 1903 article in the *Review of Reviews* by John Commons, included "all of those services which an employer may render to his work people over and above the payment of wages."[14] At the time, the term *welfare* was understood to mean well-being, prosperity, and good health. It was not until a half-century later that it took on associations related to federal programs for those in poverty.

In developing the concept of welfare work, American capitalists hoped to avoid the charitable connotations of "betterment" and "social uplift" related to government and philanthropical "handouts" to the needy. Tone observes, "Welfare work, in contrast, provided contractual embellishments to hardworking, deserving wage earners—workers who neither needed nor, according to employers, wanted state support . . . welfare capitalists insisted that self-respecting workers would not willingly prostrate themselves to the state to secure concessions they could otherwise 'earn.'"[15]

As proposals for legislated health insurance and pensions surfaced across the country during the early 1900s, welfare capitalists took peremptory action. U.S. Steel invested $5 million in employee health plans, retirement funds, and workplace safety. International Harvester followed suit with employee death, disability, and sickness benefits. George H. Perkins, a director at both United States Steel Company and International Harvester, saw government intervention as the source of, rather than the cure for, existing labor tensions. "For every ounce of trouble brought about in industry through their selfishness and cupidity of business men," he said, "a pound of trouble has been brought about through half-baked laws and muttonhead legislation on the part of our legislators. Our legislators have not even possessed hindsight, and they have been veritable babes in foresight."[16]

Large employers also considered welfare work to be profitable paternalism: strikes, absenteeism, high rates of employee turnover, and worker inefficiency were all threats to productivity—and therefore to financial gains. Modest investments in employee contentment could cut costs and raise net profits as well as garner political returns by deferring government intervention in labor relations. Consequently, welfare capitalists made investments that gave rise to highly structured working and living conditions under corporate provision and control.

The tenets of welfare capitalism extended well beyond the factory gate. Having seen the positive impact that changes in the physical work environment wrought (e.g., cafeterias, ample rest rooms, water fountains, good lighting, and improved ventilation), employers took an interest in controlling the wider social environment as well. Housing conditions, family life, and recreational pursuits were all considered to affect the quality and quantity of a worker's output, and corporations set about extending control of their workers' social environment. By imposing tight restrictions, social ills such as inadequate housing, family problems, and alcoholism could be identified and eliminated without challenging the corporate hierarchy that kept workers subordinate. "Collapsing the boundaries of home, leisure, and work, welfare work attempted to modify not only employees' work space but the totality of their environment. Acknowledging that what workers did after hours affected their work performance, welfare employers cast their reform net wide. . . . Welfare work sought to regulate and control workers' use of personal time, often making the receipt of benefits contingent on round-the-clock 'good' behavior verified with home inspections."[17]

That paternalistic philosophy served not only to control workers' lives but also to define their welfare on company terms. Instead of raising wages to allow workers themselves to determine how they would live and play, welfare employers determined that they alone knew what was best for employees. By providing housing along with parades and picnics, organized sports, theaters, YMCA buildings, and schools and churches, employers played a key role in all spheres of workers' lives, thereby increasing dependence on and loyalty to the company. Organized sports in particular had the dual function of reinforcing the concept of a "corporate team" and creating rivalries within the work force itself rather than between company and workers, thus attenuating class-consciousness among the work force.

The blandishments welfare capitalists offered workers never eliminated the possibility of using violent force against labor. At the outset of the Progressive Era, the Pinkerton National Detective Agency, "Only one of dozens of agencies specializing in the supply of spies and armed forces to employers, had more active agents and reserves in its ranks than the standing army of the United States."[18] Even after the Progressive Era was well under way, for instance, men, women, and children supporting a United Mine Workers strike in Colorado were machine-gunned and burned to death in the infamous Ludlow Massacre.

More than industrial efficiency and increased worker productivity motivated company owners to promote welfare work. Many of the largest companies to embrace welfare capitalism were those controlled by their original founders. Certainly, some were interested in maintaining the close-knit ties between management and workers or the "familylike" environment that had existed in the early days of the enterprise. Others saw it as a way to share their wealth with the workers who were responsible for it. These motives were often inspired by deep religious beliefs. In some other cases, perceived class differences and a desire to "Americanize" workers played an important role in promoting the philosophy of welfare capitalism. The prevailing belief was that many working-class individuals, both immigrants or native-born, lacked strong family values and thus needed "uplifting" or "betterment." The companies' activities were aimed at "Americanizing" workers and making their family values more wholesome. Critics of welfare work saw these efforts as cynical attempts to control workers' lives, undermine unionism, and blunt public concerns about extreme wealth.[19]

An ingrained sense of morality and "family values" was fundamental in shaping many corporate welfare work programs. George Pullman designed his town for workers to be free of "all baneful influences." The YMCA programs sponsored by International Harvester in Benham and U.S. Steel in Lynch, Kentucky, followed a practice established by the large railroads and other companies. YMCAs, many corporate leaders believed, not only provided wholesome recreational activities but also taught workers economy, thrift, and Christian values. The belief in family values brought about corporate efforts to improve family life through health care, good educational opportunities for children, home beautification programs, and recreation for all family members. These efforts are evident in Benham and Lynch, where awards were given for the best gardens, homes were inspected to ensure good maintenance, academically strong schools were provided for children, churches were constructed, and companies sponsored Fourth of July and other holiday programs for families. In some cases, however, it was company pride and not benevolence that prompted sponsorship of employee activities. "They hired and gave employment to very good baseball players and they allowed these gentlemen to work on the outside as painters, as just regular day labor, but their main job was playing baseball . . . I mean the company felt like they needed to be well represented with their baseball teams in the mountains and in the coal fields."[20]

The Benham YMCA (white), also know as the "clubhouse," housed a barber shop, pool room, ice-cream parlor, bowling alley, and theater. In the background is the Chicago House, Benham's hotel.

Nevertheless, the industrial welfare programs embedded in the very concept of a model company town were directly aimed at preventing workers from becoming class conscious and organizing trade unions. "This concern," writes Margaret Crawford, "far more than considerations of humanity, efficiency, or publicity, motivated welfare capitalism."[21] Workers themselves were clearly aware of this dynamic, as is seen from Will Herford's popular "Welfare Song" written in 1913:

> Sing a song of 'Welfare,'
> Forty 'leven kinds,
> Elevate your morals
> Cultivate your minds
> Kindergartens, nurses
> Bathtubs, books, and flowers,
> Anything but better pay,
> Or shorter working hours.[22]

The Business of Benevolence in Harlan County

Welfare capitalism, or "sociological work," was a widespread concept if not practice across the American coalfields of the early 1900s. Between 1911 and 1916 the coal industry journal *Coal Age* had a regular feature entitled the "Sociological Department," which was "devoted to the welfare of miners everywhere and especially designed for the betterment of living conditions in mining communities."[23] The column focused on the four most important concerns of the operators, each of which directly affected production and therefore profits: alcoholism, strikes, worker turnover, and safety. Robert Munn explains these concerns:

> It was felt that the only real solution would be a "total systems approach." All significant aspects of the miners' environment should be carefully planned and controlled by a benevolent and prudent employer. . . . By 1910 a number of the major coal companies had both the desire and the means to undertake the development of what became known—at least by the companies—as "model towns" . . . [and] by 1916 a number of the larger coal companies had developed comprehensive welfare programs designed to create model citizens for their model towns.[24]

Efforts were made to improve the "morals, manners and education of miners," most often through programs of recreation and worker "uplift" operated or supplemented by the industrial department of the YMCA.[25] Consequently, saloons were banned from company property, sports leagues organized, and the study of first aid and gardening was promoted through competitions and awards. Some observers approved of these programs wholeheartedly, if a bit naively: "Many of the employers are sincerely interested in the welfare and happiness of their employees, and employ experts in education, religion, recreation, and health to enlist the interest of the employees in well wrought out programs in these several fields. In such instances the opportunities for self-improvement are there for those who wish to avail themselves of them."[26] Others were more suspicious of company towns and their programs: "The best of men dread the eye that follows them night and day."[27]

Certainly, much welfare capitalism was transparent corporate self-aggrandizement. The corporate response to the perceived "liquor problem" among miners, for example, was to banish saloons and other establishments purveying alcoholic beverages from their towns. Yet when one coal operator faced the possibility of labor organizing among black miners in Alabama, "Company officials quickly dispatched a railroad car of beer and whiskey to dampen the strike fever."[28]

The story behind Benham's "colored" YMCA provides a case history of micromanagement, corporate benevolence, and racial stereotyping. The company had financed a large YMCA for whites that included, according to a local newspaper, a "modern theater building, drug department, billiard and bowling rooms, committee and lounging rooms, shower baths, and barber shop."[29] In 1913, W. A. Tucker, superintendent of mining operations in Benham, began corresponding with H. F. Perkins, president of International Harvester's steel-producing subsidiary, Wisconsin Steel, about building a "colored YMCA." At first reluctant, Perkins accepted the concept of a separate facility for blacks because "Mr. [C. H.] McCormick felt that—while perhaps they had been hasty in determining on this proposition—he had given his word and it must be carried out." In no way, however, did Perkins want it to be equal to the white facility. He thought two rooms should suffice and opined that no plumbing was necessary because black miners had access to the company bathhouse. The restrictions he placed on the size and scope of the project stemmed in part from budgetary concerns but in the main came from racial stereotypes and prejudice: "I see no reason whatever for supplying a barber shop for the negro population. I cannot imagine they would use it enough to pay for the investment before it would be ruined, to say nothing about making a return on it."[30]

Having settled on a construction budget of $4,000 and another $2,000 in equipment costs, the managers turned to staffing. After noting Tucker's observation that "a colored man is not good to boss another colored man," Perkins got down to his real concerns about the operation of the new YMCA: "It will be necessary to watch whoever is in charge of the Y.M.C.A. buildings in Benham to be sure they are not doing us any damage through disseminating ideas among our working forces which might be the foundation of dissatisfaction and sedition." Although the building was to be staffed by employees of the YMCA, Perkins nevertheless wanted the local superintendent to maintain tight control over them so that their efforts went into "channels which we all believe are desired for the people individually and for the community as a whole, as related to our business there."[31]

After the building was completed and in operation, the discussion turned to the advisability of a grand opening. Tucker cautioned against it: "I would not make any special occasion of it. . . . The Southern negro is very easily spoiled if he can be made to feel that he is in any way equal to the white man."[32] The company needed black miners and spent money on a "colored" YMCA to attract them, but those decisions did not represent any underlying notion of fairness. Rather, they were done grudgingly and with an eye to cutting corners and maintaining control, with the underlying assumption of black inferiority.

Corporate welfare as practiced in model towns affected black miners in particular. In pamphlets and newspaper articles, they were reminded that their well-being depended more on the beneficence of their corporate "parents" than on "radicalism in labor." Joe William Trotter makes this point clear: "The relationship between blacks and coal operators was mediated through the increasing rhetoric of welfare capitalism, conditioned by the operators' paternalistic and racist notions of black dependency. . . . In exchange for employment, housing, credit at the company store, and a gradually expanding variety of recreational and social welfare programs, employers expected deference from all workers, but especially from blacks."[33] Wisconsin Steel Company President Perkins expressed that perspective in discussing the "Colored YMCA" in Benham:

> I am very hopeful that this, as in the case of the other Y.M.C.A., will prove to be in the end very beneficial to the content of our people in living and working at Benham, but I realize fully that there might be a man whose moral and religious character and purpose was of the highest, who yet might have commercial or sociological views the airing of which would be very detrimental to the general principles of good business on which we are endeavoring to conduct our enterprises.[34]

Between 1910 and 1929, American industrialists had built more than forty new company towns, including Benham and Lynch. During the 1930s, President Franklin D. Roosevelt's New Deal Administration set about evaluating the physical, social, and economic impacts of those towns through the auspices of its National Resource Planning Board. The board was biased toward community planning but suspicious of paternalism and corporate ownership; nevertheless, its overall appraisal was positive. It found, for instance, that the housing in company towns was larger, better built, and more affordable than in other towns and that company towns were the sites of cohesive and unified communities with identities distinct from those of the local factory or mine.[35]

The brief era of model towns and corporate welfare in the Appalachian coalfields ended as suddenly as it had appeared and for many of the same reasons. When it became no longer economically necessary to attract and retain miners, coal operators stopped building company towns and closed their industrial welfare programs in existing towns. Beginning about 1920, the coal industry started to accumulate surplus inventory, faced lower prices for its product, and experienced stronger competition from alternative fuels like oil and natural gas. By 1926 the economic slump caused employment in the Appalachian coalfields to decline. With dwindling profits and an uncertain future, the industry also initiated cutbacks in capital investments such as company towns and in the operating costs associated with welfare programs. Moreover, union organizers had laid to rest the widespread belief that corporate benevolence was a company's best insurance against labor unrest. For the most part, by 1930 coal operators considered development of new mining towns as nonessential and the operation of social programs as ineffective for their purposes. Corporate community-building and welfare capitalism flourished in the Appalachian coalfields for nearly three decades before widespread unionization and the depression of the 1930s challenged their viability. We will next explore the results of these industrial policies as they were implemented in two towns situated at the foot of Black Mountain, Benham and Lynch.

CHAPTER 5

✼ ✼ ✼ "Living Tolerably Well Together":
Life in Model Towns along
Looney Creek

The opening of the Harlan County coalfields came when the L&N Railroad completed the Wasiota and Black Mountain Branch of its rail lines into the county in the early 1900s. By 1921 Harlan had become the top coal-producing county in Kentucky. The coal operations established by International Harvester at Benham in 1910 and United States Steel at Lynch seven years later ultimately became the largest in the county. The two towns also became thriving communities that fluctuated in size as the need for coal, and therefore labor, rose and fell. Ample evidence of their origins as model towns can be found in Benham and Lynch today. A company store, mine buildings, theater, schools, and homes—some in use and good repair, others boarded up and falling into ruin—dot the roadside and extend up the hills.[1]

It was the demand for coke used in the companies' steel furnaces that led to the founding of these towns. Benham was first, founded when the International Harvester Company came to Harlan County to mine the rich coal seams under Black Mountain. Ten years earlier, the Deering Harvester Company (later to become the International Harvester Company) had decided to build a steel mill in South Chicago; it set up Benham's coal-mining operations to provide a steady flow of raw materials at reasonable prices. The steel mill was completed in 1908 and operated by a subsidiary, the Wisconsin Steel Company.[2] Two years later, the subsidiary company set up a sawmill next to Looney Creek, where virgin timber from Black Mountain was planed for building a self-contained company town. The L&N Railroad extended a spur from Pineville, Kentucky, to Benham, and in September 1911 the first load of coal was shipped from Benham to Chicago. According to the *Harlan Daily Enterprise*, "By November 1912, 300 coke ovens were completed, 175 houses, the town was lighted by electricity, water works were under way, three churches were built, a school with an attendance of 130, and a well-equipped Y.M.C.A. building was opened."[3]

The valley was later described as having hillsides "as steep as a horse's face."[4] Consequently, Benham was designed in the form of a circle, with mine offices, company store, hospital, theater, schools, and churches at the center and eventually 520 company-owned homes lining the short streets running up the slopes from the valley. The Yowell Post Office, which sat on the site, was renamed Benham after a mountain that rose above the new company town.[5]

The building of Lynch by the United States Steel Company followed in 1917 after the company purchased forty thousand acres at the head of Looney Creek to start its coal-mining operations. A subsidiary, the United States Coal and Coke Company, began construction of a town and opened a mine shaft in August of that year to provide coal for U.S. Steel's mills in Gary, Indiana. Because the L&N Railroad refused to extend its spur up Looney Creek from Benham, supplies had to be hauled upstream by wagon to build the new town. Named after Thomas Lynch, the first president of the United States Coal and Coke Company, the model town took more than eight years to complete.[6] Memphis Tennessee Garrison, a black welfare worker in U.S. Steel's West Virginia mining operations, notes, "But now U.S. Steel had the best houses; they had the safest mines. They had the most modern mining machinery and they set the pace."[7]

Lynch was laid out in six sections along Looney Creek, with the first section downstream closest to Benham and the last at the farthest point upstream. The long, narrow town filled the valley floor and spread up both hillsides. The mine portals, tipple, offices, store, schools, and other buildings housing mine operations were at the center of the town. Housing for the work force included two hundred single homes, four hundred double homes, and five boardinghouses with twenty-two bedrooms each for unmarried employees. A hotel with 108 bedrooms was built to accommodate visiting company officials and others needing temporary housing. A fifty-four-bed hospital, power plant, churches, and recreational facilities were also constructed.[8]

Lynch Hotel under construction, 1920.

A third town in the area, Poor Fork, had been settled during the 1820s at the confluence of Looney Creek and the Poor Fork of the Cumberland River. Mention of Poor Fork first appears in the census in 1870 with a population of fifty, mostly farmers. The Louisville and Nashville Railroad came up the Cumberland River valley in the late 1800s, fostering Poor Fork's growth when it was designated a watering stop for L&N steam engines. In 1895 the town was incorporated, and by the early 1900s it was the site of a short-lived timber boom. The town later became a railhead of the L&N Railroad for the spurs that served the mining operations in Benham and Lynch. The prosperity of the two model mining communities caused Poor Fork's residents to reconsider their town's name, and in 1926 they changed it to Cumberland. Because of their proximity and locations along Looney Creek, the histories and economies of Cumberland, Benham, and Lynch have been closely intertwined for most of the twentieth century.[9]

The Work Force

From the beginning, the towns of Benham and Lynch were to be model coal communities. International Harvester set out to provide "a pleasant community" for its work force, with the goal of attracting "good men and keeping them" as company employees.[10] U.S. Steel's effort was described as "bending every resource of large capital and the trained intelligence which money can buy to the making of a modern town."[11] Although Benham was established earlier, by the mid-1920s both towns were thriving communities that competed with each other for workers, on athletic fields, and in matters of community pride. The competition to attract and keep employees, and later to avoid unionism, brought numerous benefits to employees and their families in the form of good schools, recreational activities, health care, and an overall quality of life enjoyed by coal miners in only a few other company towns. This lasted until the 1930s, when relations between the competing unions and between workers and the respective companies turned violent, resulting in the mine wars of "bloody Harlan County." Lynch miners ultimately were organized by the United Mine Workers of America (UMWA), and Benham miners joined the Progressive Mine Workers of America (PMWA).

Residents were drawn to the towns by the availability of jobs. They came by train and on horses and mules, some on foot. They moved into company-owned houses, shopped at company-owned stores, worshiped in churches built by the companies, sent their children to schools supported by the companies, and participated in company-sponsored sports and recreational activities. Street maintenance, health care, water and electricity, fire and police protection, the cemetery, and other community services were also company-provided. Charles Gregory moved to Benham in 1921 after his discharge from the army, although his mother objected to his decision. "I came to Benham anyway and was I surprised! Churches, Y.M.C.A., schools, everything you would find in any other ordinary small town. I got a job in the Y.M.C.A. and worked until . . . I went inside (underground) to load coal."[12]

Life was good in Benham and Lynch, but it was clear to everyone that International Harvester and U.S. Steel owned and operated the towns and set the rules in each community. The sense of "belonging" to the company is captured in an article in *Coal Mines: Benham,* an International Harvester magazine: "At Benham, when a miner ends his day's work, he goes home to a house built by Harvester. Water from Harvester's modern filtration plant quenches his thirst. His wife shops in a Harvester store. His children receive their education in a school built by Harvester. Should he fall sick, Harvester doctors in a Harvester hospital care for him. Even his Sunday worship is offered in a church provided by the Company."[13]

Unable to fill their burgeoning labor needs from the local area, both companies actively recruited miners and other skilled workers to come to the Black Mountain area. Company agents met incoming immigrants at Ellis Island, hired them, gave them travel funds, and sent them to Kentucky in groups accompanied by an interpreter to aid in the journey. These "ethnics," as they came to be called, included Hungarians, Austrians, Serbs, Poles, Greeks, Italians, and others from Eastern and Mediterranean Europe. Some immigrants who first settled in Chicago or Pittsburgh were also recruited to work in the mining operations. "Oh, they were like a melting pot. I can remember the Italians playing bocci ball at the bowling alley, I can remember the Hungarians having ethnic dances where they hung grapes from the ceiling, pods of grapes, and played Hungarian music. There were Slavish . . . there were Spaniards, Russians, just a potpourri of ethnics," Bill Bosch recalled.[14]

Other company agents were sent south into the industrial regions of Virginia and Northern Alabama and the cotton fields of Georgia, Alabama, and Mississippi to recruit African Americans. One company agent, remembered by the name "Limehouse," was legendary in his ability to sneak sharecroppers away from the white land-owners at night by hiding recruits and their families behind stacks of vegetable boxes on his truck. "When the coal companies first started," Dorothy Morrow remembered, "there was a man, I don't know his nationality, but his name was Limehouse. He would go to Alabama and get these strong, healthy, black men who were working in fields, maybe some were working in mines, I don't know. He would bring them to Lynch and Benham to work in the coal companies, . . . He would bring the men up and then make return trips and bring the wives, children, dogs or whatever, so this is one way I know that a lot of black people got here." Other black men, hearing of the job opportunities through family networks, made their way to Benham and Lynch, usually sending for their families after earning enough for the trip. Johnnie Jones sent for his wife and three children, who were still in Alabama, as soon as he could. "I sent for 'em, I sent for 'em after I made me a good payday, I sent for 'em. And my ole lady and children, I met her in Harlan." Because of the fluctuating labor force and because both communities were unincorporated, it is difficult to assess the exact population sizes. At peak employment times, however, Benham's population was estimated at about three thousand people and Lynch's at more than six thousand.[15]

Descriptions of the work force suggest that its composition changed over time. Initially, in Lynch, the majority of outside workers were native-born Americans recruited from the local area, whereas underground miners were mostly "foreign-born and colored," according to T. E. Johnson. "The labor force during the first year was truly a colorful group of all types, creeds and colors." One magazine article in 1926 described Lynch as the "new melting pot" and estimated that "approximately twenty-five percent of the population of Lynch was American-born white with the rest being Negro and Eastern European."[16] Henrietta Sweatt, who came to Lynch in 1923 to teach at the Lynch Colored School, described the diversity of the work force: "When I first came here, there were as many blacks and foreigners as there were whites. They were from Italy, Austria, and all those places."[17]

Johnson reports that when the elementary school for whites opened in 1921, about 75 percent of its students were children of immigrant workers. The Bank of Lynch featured a foreign exchange department so that foreign-born employees could transact business with their home countries. "By the end of 1920," according to Johnson, "the la-

Henrietta Sweatt's first-grade class.

bor force was fairly stable, as a great many of the employees had moved their families to Lynch and most of the foreign-born employees kept boarders of their own nationality. The Americans, both white and colored, and the foreign employees worked and lived in harmony. Each had his own church services, fraternal organizations, celebrations, and social affairs. The only segregation requirements were separate housing, dining, amusement, school, and bath house facilities for the colored."[18]

In the depths of the Great Depression, the Lynch mines operated only four or five days a month. As a result, large numbers of foreign-born miners migrated north in search of employment. "I don't know what caused so many foreigners to leave, but they did," said Sweatt.[19] U.S. Steel sent recruiters into the local area and into Georgia and Alabama to bolster its work force, offering new hires work clothes and a new set of tools. In 1938 the Lynch operations employed about 2,500 individuals, including "57 percent white Americans, 7 percent foreign born, and 36 percent colored," a definite turnaround from earlier years.[20]

Union Organizing

Not surprisingly, unions tried to organize the work force in both communities. Much of the strife over unionization in Harlan County initially occurred near mines in the central part of the county along the Martin Fork and Clover Fork tributaries of the Cumberland River. Only after these union locals were established did the push for unionization reach into the eastern end of the county to mines located along the Poor Fork. That may account for why the mines at Benham and Lynch, where a majority of the black miners in the county were employed, were not organized by the United Mine Workers until 1937.

There is also evidence that the large, absentee-owned mining operations such as those of International Harvester and U.S. Steel were more resistant to unions than the smaller, locally owned mines clustered in the center of Harlan County. One tactic that large corporate owners used was the formation of token unions. The Union of Lynch Employees, founded and controlled by U.S. Steel from 1933 until 1938,

First meeting of Lynch United Mine Workers of America local, 1937.

is a good example of this ploy, as was the Benham Employees Association.[21]

During 1935, however, more direct measures were used to resist UMW organizing efforts in Lynch. At that time the police chief, Joseph R. Menefee, and his thirteen deputies were all paid and armed by the company. John Hevener has described their actions: "During the union campaign, Lynch officers barred organizers from company property, maintained surveillance of the state highway that passed through the town, sounded their automobile horns to drown out [union] sound trucks, and followed union members from door to door destroying union literature. . . . Union membership at Lynch which had risen from one hundred to seventeen hundred during the brief campaign, quickly receded once the organizers were forced to withdraw."[22]

In 1933 the "in-house" union at Lynch negotiated a contract with U.S. Steel covering "working conditions and matters pertaining to industrial relations." That contract continued in place until 1937, when, under pressure of organizing efforts by the United Mine Workers of America, the company agreed to a new contract with the Union of Lynch Employees and UMWA. The 1937 contract included a clause stating that if UMWA membership reached a majority of employees, they would be declared the sole bargaining agent. By 1939 the Progressive Mine Workers of America and UMWA were competing for the right to represent the miners in Lynch. When UMWA succeeded in enrolling 57 percent of the work force there they were recognized as the sole bargaining agent. One company manager, however, commented that UMWA's success was due to their "rough and tumble methods of organizing."[23] When they lost in Lynch, the PMWA turned its efforts to organizing the International Harvester work force in Benham, at which it was successful.

Both companies tried to prevent unionization through better labor relations and intimidation. When asked about union organizing, Woolford Griffey, a Benham resident and the first African American miner promoted to mine foreman by International Harvester, recalled, "If you were working for, or if it was reported you were working for a union, you couldn't live in the company houses long, cause they'd fire you and run you off." "I didn't belong to the union [at] first," said Alfonso

Simms, who lived in Lynch. "They didn't go for no union man . . . the company, didn't want no union either." Not belonging to the union could be just as difficult: "If somebody caught you and you weren't a union man they'd baptize you in the name of John L. Lewis. . . . They'd drag you down to a creek bank, hold you under water, and ask if you believed in John L. They didn't drown nobody. They just held them under water until they said they believed."[24]

Unionization did not prevent work stoppages. The first strike by Lynch miners occurred in April 1939 and lasted more than six weeks. There were five wildcat strikes in Lynch during 1941 and six during 1942 and 1943. Labor unrest in the two communities was finally put on hold during the remaining years of World War II due to legislative and executive action by the federal government. After the war, tensions continued to mount between the companies and the unions and also between the two unions as they attempted to organize other workers. "They had big shootouts back then, yeah, everywhere in the coalfields was kinda violent . . . you were subject to get killed, or ran off, at least ran off, or beat up," Woolford Griffey recalls. The county continued to be known in the late 1940s as "Bloody Harlan" because of the turmoil of the "union wars." In spite of the violence, Benham and Lynch provided residents with a sense community that is still looked upon favorably by those who lived there. Eddie McDonald, like many other current and former residents, remembers fondly, "There were good relationships between people there at that time and that is what helped mold us for what we have encountered through our lives, that small community, what it brought out of us."[25]

Housing and Health Care

Housing provided by the company generally consisted of four- or five-room homes. In Lynch, the majority were built as two-family units to save land. Twelve different home plans were used to provide variety, and buildings were painted different colors to avoid a monotonous "coal camp look." The homes were rented to married employees, and single men lived in boardinghouses or the hotel. In 1925 a worker in Lynch who lived in a five-room house would pay about $12.25 a month rent—

$2 per room, $1.50 for electricity, and 75 cents for water. Residents were required to keep their homes and yards neat and clean, with some maintenance provided by the company. "Since Lynch was a captive coal town, . . . you lived in a company house," says Bill Bosch. "There were several varieties of those houses, but they all had outhouses at that time. . . . of course, the company in that day did a good job because they painted those houses and they did the upkeep on them."[26]

Both towns enjoyed modern infrastructures, with many paved streets, electricity, complete sewer systems and clean water supplies, and up-to-date heating systems. About thirty homes in Lynch, set aside for management, had inside plumbing and central heating, and the remainder had outside toilets connected to septic tanks. "Warm Morning" stoves heated the homes with stoker or block coal.[27] In Benham and Lynch, residents purchased coal for home heating by placing an order with the payroll office. Rent and a charge for the coal were then subtracted from the miner's paycheck.[28] If a worker lost his job or quit

Eight-room double house, Lynch, 1919.

Homes in Lynch.

the company, he and his family were expected to vacate the company's house immediately. Although that requirement reinforced the company-town image for Benham and Lynch, residents still developed a feeling of belonging and sense of community and had pride in their respective towns.

The companies also provided health care for employees and their families and operated schools for their children. A fully staffed medical clinic and hospital were built in each community to treat work-related injuries and provide up-to-date health care and support. The hospitals were staffed with physicians and nurses who were also company employees. Although white and black employees and their families were treated at the clinics and hospitals, wards for in-patients were racially separated. Because of the medical services available in Benham and Lynch, a spinal meningitis epidemic that raged across the mountains and through much of the southeastern United States in 1936 caused fewer fatalities in the two towns than in nearby communities. In Lynch, for example, the death rate was just 6 percent of those who

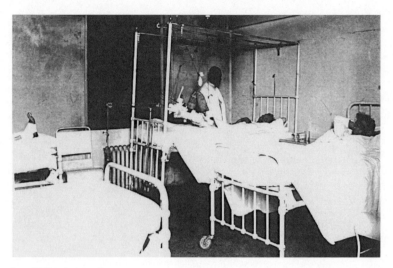

Lynch Hospital ward.

had the disease, whereas mortality rates in other southeastern Kentucky communities were as high as 95 percent. The low mortality rates were due in large part to administration of an antitoxin to employees and their families at no cost to them as well as to precautionary health measures that the medical staff put in place.[29]

The Company Store

Mainstream America's perception of life in coal towns has been shaped, in part, by musicians like Merle Travis and Tennessee Ernie Ford, who sang about owing "my soul to the company store." The company store was, indeed, a central aspect of life for most residents of Benham and Lynch. As Dorothy Morrow remembered the one in Lynch, "We had what they consider now a shopping center, we had it all in one building, so did Benham. Anything you wanted was at that one store. So you had no need to travel nowhere to buy anything—clothing, food, furniture, appliances—everything was sold under one roof. It was called the company commissary. But it was really a recent facsimile of the shopping centers, or the malls or whatever they might call it."[30]

Woolford Griffey also recalled that "everybody" traded at the Benham company store. "When I first started in the mine, if you worked for that company, you either traded there—they had paper script, books, as they called it, . . . the only way you could use it was to trade at the company store, unless some other merchant wanted to take a chance on it." "One could buy anything at the Company Store from a straight pin to a Cadillac car," said Mattye Knight.[31] Both stores still stand. The one in Lynch is vacant, but the building in Benham has been restored and houses the Kentucky Coal Mining Museum.

Schools and Churches

By the mid-1920s, each town enjoyed the benefits of strong, albeit segregated, schools, which were operated as private facilities separate from the county school district. The Benham white and black high schools were housed in modern buildings. As described in a press release intended for publication in the *Harlan Daily Enterprise,* the white high school was constructed under the direct supervision of C. F. Biggert, the mine superintendent, and "lacks almost nothing to make it a perfect physical plant to serve its purpose. An equally well equipped and built school for the colored is also provided, . . . which is surpassed by no school in the state for colored."[32]

Initially, children of the U.S. Steel employees attended schools in Benham with the children of International Harvester employees. By the beginning of the decade, 850 were enrolled in the Lynch schools, which had nine white and two black teachers. At first there were numerous problems with employee turnover and the fact that English was not the native language of many students. By 1928 both companies had constructed school buildings for white and black students. That year in Lynch, about nine hundred students were enrolled in the white school, and 450 were enrolled in the black school.[33]

Competition existed for good teachers, just as it did at other levels between the two companies. Black teachers who had graduate degrees from Howard, Tuskegee, Fisk, and other prominent black colleges received bonuses and competitive wages to teach in Benham and Lynch. Kentucky State College (now University) was the source of the ma-

Lynch High School graduates.

jority of black teachers in the schools of eastern Kentucky. Mattye Knight moved from Frankfort, Kentucky, to teach in 1945 because "the wages for teachers in Lynch Colored School were good—among the highest in the state."[34] These well-trained teachers often spent their summers studying at the University of Chicago, University of Wis-

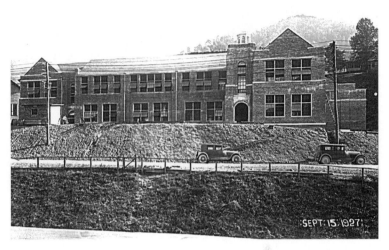

Benham High School (white), 1927.

consin, Columbia University, and other premier institutions of higher education.[35]

The high school curricula for both black and white students included courses in English, mathematics, science, foreign languages, and history. Many graduates of both the black and white high schools attended college after graduation. "I would say for the teachers here in this school, they were black teachers, you certainly had to learn, they made sure that you learned," recalled Andrea Massey. "The teachers cared about you, making sure that you worked and that you understood before you left, that was their goal." Gean Austin remembers that the teachers were "just like a part of the family to you." The value placed on education is evident in the fact that several of the old school buildings are still in use. The white school in Benham is now a bed and breakfast, and the black school building is used as an office building for the current coal mine operator. The black school building in Lynch is used by the Lynch Chapter of the Eastern Kentucky Social Club for its monthly

Lynch Colored Public School, now the Eastern Kentucky Social Club chapter club-house.

meetings. On weekends—especially during the Memorial Day holiday—the facility is used as a social gathering place, a dance hall, what William Turner calls "a throwback to the typical rural south juke joint."[36]

The companies' reach extended even into the religious life of employees and their families. Churches in Benham and Lynch were built and owned by the company; U.S. Steel contributed the land and half of the cost of construction. The Community Church for white families and the Mt. Sinai Baptist Church for black families were the first to be built in Lynch. At the same time, plans were prepared for building the Roman Catholic Church of the Resurrection. By 1924 two other church buildings, Goode Temple African Methodist Episcopal Church and St. Nicholas Eastern Rite Orthodox (Greek Orthodox), were underway. "Lynch had numerous denominations, Methodists, Baptists, they had black churches, and, of course, my church was the Catholic Church," remembers Bill Bosch. Coal operators supported worship in many forms. When Billy Sunday visited the area in July 1922,

Lynch Mt. Sinai Church. Cecil Mullins and family (left) and Leon
Walters and family (right) with the Rev. J. R. Boyd (rear).

the companies allowed employees, including mine crews, to leave their
jobs for two hours to attend the outdoor services.[37]

Recreation

Recreational facilities and activities also played a key role in each town.
Sponsored by the companies, the activities encompassed first-run
movies, concerts, traveling vaudeville shows, dances, bowling, and
sports. International Harvester employees had a 50 cent monthly fee
for the Benham Amusement Association deducted from their pay-
checks. In Lynch, the Victory Building, also known as the Y, housed

Lynch Amusement Building (also called the Victory Building), which housed the
Victory Theater, a restaurant that served blacks and whites in separate dining rooms,
a barber shop, bowling alleys, pool tables, and a dance and lodge hall.

bowling alleys, a theater, pool room, restaurant, and rooms for danc-
ing and lodge meetings.[38] Separate dances for black and white residents
were held regularly in the Victory Building. The companies brought
prominent black entertainers such as Cab Calloway and Louis Arm-
strong to eastern Kentucky for shows and dances.[39]

The companies also encouraged ethnic organizations, clubs, and
lodge groups. Among these were the Croatian Club, Italian-American
Club, and Serbian Club as well as black and white fraternal organizations. The companies sponsored parades on the Fourth of July and
Labor Day, followed by activities and treats for the children. In Benham, the company sponsored the Kentucky Travelers, a well-known
local black quintet. Members of the group would use their vacation
time to tour other states, singing harmony and spirituals.[40]

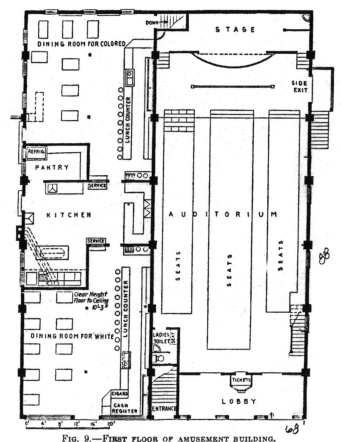

FIG. 9.—FIRST FLOOR OF AMUSEMENT BUILDING.

Construction drawings for the Lynch Amusement Building.

Sports were very popular leisure activities for both participants and fans. After International Harvester opened a nine-hole golf course just outside of Benham, U.S. Steel built a seven-hole course in Lynch, requiring two holes to be played twice to complete a nine-hole round. Both companies also sponsored highly competitive bowling teams that seemed to be perpetual opponents. All four high schools (white and black) fielded teams in football, men's and women's basketball, baseball, and track. The companies made sure that the teams had good

A costume dance.

equipment and coaching. Like most coal towns of the period, International Harvester and U.S. Steel sponsored baseball teams composed of company employees, and athletic skill was at times more important in securing employment than job skills above- or belowground. U.S. Steel reserved aboveground, "outside" work to recruit baseball players for the white Lynch Bulldogs, later named the Lynch Steelers, and for the African American Lynch Grays. The Lynch baseball stadium, which also was used for circuses, carnivals, and other special events, was completed in 1919.

Competition to hire the best ballplayers was strong. Willie Watts's father, a black miner from Alabama and an excellent hitter and fielder, was recruited for the Benham team by a manager tired of losing bets to his counterpart at other coal companies. William Bosch recalls conversations between his father and other miners about men hired as carpenters, painters, and in other above-ground positions at Lynch with the stipulation they would be released if they did not make the baseball team. U.S. Steel employee files note three such terminations in 1937.

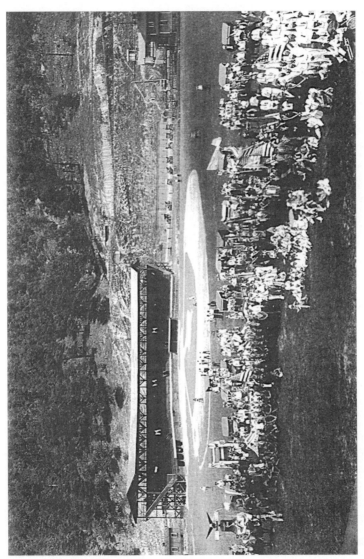

Lynch ballfield after Fourth of July Parade, 1926.

Lynch Pirates with Coach John V. Coleman, mid-1950s.

The notations state simply "Carpenter, supposed to be ball player, couldn't make team. Cut off as agreed with mgr [*sic*]."[41] Each town had a good baseball field, and the stands were usually filled for games of both the black and white baseball teams. "We had a big stadium down here in Benham and they had one up there in Lynch, a grand stand stadium," Woolford Griffey remembers. "I've seen crowds down there as high as, oh, six or seven hundred people," he said. A Lynch Ball Club season ticket to attend both "white ball games" and "colored ball games" cost $5 and admitted "one man, wife and all their children under 16 yrs. old." Bill Bosch notes that the stands were always filled by black and white fans for the games of both teams. Several players from Lynch teams were drafted by and played for major league teams.[42] With this general background in mind, we now turn to a closer look at how African Americans who worked and lived along Looney Creek experienced daily life.

CHAPTER 6

❦ ❦ ❦   "What Kept You Standing,
        Why Didn't You Fall?":
        African Americans in Benham
        and Lynch

The literature about coal towns in Appalachia presents a mixed view
of life in these communities. The conventional view is that of a harsh,
bleak existence under the dictatorial rule of mine operators. Ron Eller
and David Corbin as well as several writers of fiction and popular song
have suggested that life was brutal in many towns owned or controlled
by coal companies. Popular reactions to the bleak life in camps range
from Mother Jones, who vowed to bring the coal barons to the attention of the Almighty when she passed on to her reward, to an English
visitor who fumed "of all the God-forsaken spots I have visited, American mining camps are certainly the worst."[1] Others, such as Crandall
Shifflett, Mary LaLone, and Price Fishback, writing more recently, por-
tray a different community. Although those who lived in the towns
faced serious social problems and physical hazards, many have fond
memories of their lives there.[2] In some coal towns people made a good
"life apart from the scrutiny and control of operators," writes Shifflett.
Helen Lewis, a sociologist, observes that although some residents remember the towns as "gossipy, dirty places with no privacy," others
remember them as "busy, booming towns in good times, with lots of
friendly, helpful neighbors."[3]

    We cannot generalize about all coal towns based on the experiences
of residents in only two model ones. What is certain, however, is that
members of the Eastern Kentucky Social Club fondly remember their
lives in Benham and Lynch as well as in Cumberland and other near-

by communities. Gean Austin, for example, expressed positive feelings about living and working in Lynch:

> Well, I'd say that it is hard to put into words, when you come from a place like Alabama where you don't have anything and you are working for somebody else and you come to a place like this in the coal mine where it seems like everybody white or black are equal and they are tied together because they are all facing the same dangers in life and it makes them a lot closer. This area here is one close community, white and black, cause everybody knows each other and they depend on each other and that's the only way you're going to survive here.[4]

Many members of the Eastern Kentucky Social Club spent their youths and early adulthoods in Benham and Lynch during the late 1930s, through the 1940s, and into the early 1950s. By that time the towns were well established, most of the infrastructure and services were in place, and most unionizing efforts had been completed even though there was still labor strife. Further, geography and company influence isolated many who lived along Looney Creek from the various social pressures and difficulties faced by blacks and whites outside the area. Throughout the depression, the strikes and shutdowns, and the disruption of World War II, U.S. Steel and International Harvester extended credit at company stores and continued to provide schooling, health care, and other services to miners and their families. Despite the turmoil of the period and control exerted by the companies, life was good for most who lived there.

A rather idyllic story about life in Benham appeared in International Harvester's company magazine in 1951. "The people of Benham," it maintained, "work together, play together, worship together. There's unity and solidarity among them. They share October beans and garden flowers. They share happiness and heartache. They meet in church, the school, the PTA, the store and in Scout work. The people of Benham live together, twenty-four hours a day."[5] Although clearly written to promote the company's self-image, most of those who lived along Looney Creek would agree that there was a sense of community and good neighborliness in the two towns. "Our neighbors were our parents as well," Della Watts said. "If my mother had to go out of town or whatever, it wasn't a matter of her trying to find a babysitter, she knew that the next door neighbor would watch out for us, make sure we went to school on time, make sure we had food to eat, and watch us until our daddy got home from the coal mine." Mattye Knight, who moved to Lynch in 1945 to teach at the Lynch Colored School, recalled that the "sense of neighborliness was unbelievable." As William Turner, who also grew up in Lynch, put it, "The vast majority of us were well fed and adequately clothed and more than decently schooled and churched. We had what to me were happy families, all living 'tolerably well together,' there, at the foot of Black Mountain."[6]

Early Experiences

The memories and values of the Eastern Kentucky Social Club members were shaped by their childhood sense of family, community security, and educational experiences. U.S. Steel and International Harvester may have been paternalistic and controlling, but they did take care of loyal workers and their families. Even during strikes and walkouts, companies extended credit at company stores to workers. "But I guess the reason a lot of people would say that they [the companies] were good, which they were, is they looked out for their community," said Gean Austin. "There used to be a lot of strikes in the coal mines so maybe you'd work six months out of the year and you were off six months out of the year. Basically, back in the thirties and forties that's how it was, but as long as you had a job, on the payroll, you could go to the store every day if you had kids and get something and just pay it whenever you went back to work, so they basically took care of you."[7] Thus, economic security—although it came with the price of following company rules at work and at home—provided a sense of well-being that extended to most of the children who lived in the two company towns.

Even young children saw coal companies as positive forces. Bill Bosch, whose father immigranted to the United States, remembers that U.S. Steel was "such a good, good company as far as people perceived them to be. Every holiday they would have a gigantic parade through town and they would have beautiful floats and they would meet in the ballpark and [it] would go on all day long. They would pass out candies and ice cream and they would have contests and it was unbelievable how they treated the coal miners' kids."[8] This meant that those who did their jobs well and did not cause trouble in the community could take care of their families during good times and bad.

The popular notion that "it takes a village to raise a child" was evident in Benham and Lynch. The entire community watched over its children. "There wasn't any crime. Because everybody had their eyes on you and if you got out of line that parent would chastise you or tell your parents. You didn't want them to tell parents, you better listen and obey those people that were talking to you. You always respected that elder person, whoever he was. It was yes sir, no ma'am. This is what we were taught," said Eddie McDonald about growing up in Benham.[9] Of course, some youths did manage to get into trouble. One such incident demonstrates the company's influence in local matters and its control over family life. In a letter to the Harlan County Courts, the Wisconsin Steel Company requested that a young man caught robbing the company store be sent to reform school "not only for his own good but for the good of the community at large." Four months later the company sent another letter, requesting his release to his father.[10]

Education

The residents' sense of well-being was reinforced through a strong school system staffed with well-qualified and caring teachers even though schools practiced the racially "separate but equal" policy enforced throughout Kentucky. Well-educated and competent teachers were recruited to teach in both the white and "colored" schools. Former teacher Mattye Knight believes the schools provided a "web and network" for the black community: "The school in Lynch was the pride of the community. The black teachers were, in fact more prepared than those at the other end of town. . . . and we had the very best students. The people stuck with the school because they wanted their kids to have better things than they did." Gean Austin has many positive memories of his teachers: "The teachers were like family to you. They stayed in the community and associated with you every day . . . you enjoyed going to school because the teachers really made it pleasant and you learned." Academic and disciplinary standards were high; teachers made sure that students learned. Their goal was "you're going to stay here and you're going to get it. You're not leaving here until you know everything I've taught you," said Andrea Massey.[11]

What is unmistakable from these comments is that raising and educating children in Lynch and Benham was a communitywide responsibility and effort. That level of caring and devotion on the part of parents and teachers, and in some respects the two companies, created a sheltered environment for youngsters growing up there. Combined with stable family values and parents' strong work ethic, these experiences make it easy to understand why members of the Eastern Kentucky Social Club have strong self-esteem and cherish memories of their days in Benham and Lynch.

Race Relations

Race relations in Benham and Lynch were far from perfect, but there was a sense of harmony and unity among blacks, whites, and the various ethnic groups that lived in the two towns. Although certain jobs, such as that of coal-loader, were set aside for blacks, mine workers in general were treated equally belowground. Aboveground, however, the state's segregation laws were in effect, and the separate but equal dictum guided both companies in almost every aspect of management. There were separate washhouse areas for white and black workers, separate school systems, and separate recreation and leisure activities; moreover, blacks lived in designated sections of each town and whites in other sections. Public dining rooms, movie theaters, dance halls, and hospital wards also were separated on the basis of race. Even International Harvester's company magazine informally carried "separate but equal" coverage of white and black workers. If an article appeared about those graduating from the white high school or about the company-sponsored white baseball team, one also appeared about the black graduates or black baseball team. Even so, a sense of solidarity among workers and their families crossed racial lines and was broken only by union versus anti-union sentiments and a local class structure based on position within the company.

Della Watts's and Gean Austin's comments on race relations are instructive. "We didn't look at it as being segregated," said Watts. "My daddy worked in the coal mines and my mother was a domestic housekeeper, she was a cook for a doctor . . . and we played with the doctor's children. We went to the show together and they sat in one area and we sat in another but we would meet up after we got out of the show." Austin was aware that state segregation laws existed, but they did not stop black and white youngsters from playing together when he was growing up. He noted, however, that "you went to different schools and churches."[12] Eddie McDonald recalled that whites and blacks in Benham mixed freely and respected each other:

> Well, to tell you the truth, me personally, I never had any problem with the white people, most of the blacks settled with themselves and the whites settled with themselves. We had one store and there weren't any partiality that I had seen growing up that if you were in line to get waited on you got waited on, if you were next, you were next, they didn't say get over here and wait on the white people. . . . during my time during the forties they had their own respectful place and we had our own respectful place but we never had any problems whatsoever with the white people there and we didn't start nothing and they didn't start anything.[13]

Bill Bosch, who grew up in one of Lynch's white ethnic families, remembered playing baseball with black friends despite efforts by "plant protection" to break up the games. "In fact, they tried to squelch it many, many times. We would play softball against them. There would be an all-black team against an all-white team, and suddenly, the cops— as I said, plant protection—would show up and . . . break up the game. . . . I feel that came down from the superintendent of the mines. The company, evidently, did not want the white kids playing with the black kids. Now, why they did that is beyond me."[14]

Bosch's observation about company management harboring racist views is perceptive. While to the outside the company demonstrated benign tolerance for all workers—black and white, native and foreign— on the inside management held the stereotypical views of most Americans at the time. It is in the confidential company correspondence that expressions of racism are found. In an internal office memo recommending against a donation to a black college, black ministers in Benham are described as a "liberal corps" and "somewhat of a nuisance." In other correspondence about construction of the "colored" YMCA building, company officials express stereotypical views about blacks, arguing in one letter that the proposed YMCA "is a wholly unnecessary facility for that class of men, in my judgment."[15]

Bosch also recognized that the black and white school facilities and recreational programs were equal in quality although company homes and churches used by black families were not as well constructed as those for white families. "They lived in their neighborhood on a back street and we knew that we lived in our neighborhood on a front street . . . their churches probably were not constructed as well as the white community churches," he said. Bosch also recalled some rivalry between black and white youths. On the way to school, whites walked east and blacks walked west, "so somewhere about midway between our schools the sidewalks became a battleground," he said. "Nobody would give, the younger kids would walk with the older kids and then it would become a shoving match." He also remembered a few rock-throwing incidents on some nights when returning from the movies.[16]

Belowground, however, companies sought to maintain good working relations between black and white workers. "They didn't go too much for oppression, you might say, in a way of speaking," said Woolford Griffey. "The big company didn't. Because we've had some incidents where a foreman would get into it with somebody, would have a remark concerning color. If you went to the right people with the right talk, then something was done about it. The person had to straighten up or leave." As William Earl Turner remembers, "We'd mix real good on the job; we'd work together and buddy together, whites and blacks, Poles, Italians, Hungarians; but when you came outside was when you saw the difference." Even with their emphasis on good racial relations on the job, however, companies did not appoint black supervisors until the 1970s. Turner was one of the black miners to file a lawsuit in 1970 to force U.S. Steel to appoint a black foreman. "Being black held me back," he said. "Everybody knows that. I should have been a mine foreman twenty-five or thirty years before anybody was. I was capable of being one. I had my papers. Some white boys came up and got the job." Gean Austin was one of the first blacks to become a supervisor in the

Lynch mine, and Woolford Griffey became the first black foreman at the mine operation in Benham. "He had a hard time getting to be foreman," Lacey Griffey said about her husband. "I remember he wanted to take the test a long time before he was able to, so I feel like they kind of kept him from it for awhile. But he was determined, so he made it."[17]

A coal town's hierarchy extended into education and other areas of the community. Although there was great racial and ethnic diversity within the ranks of miners and aboveground hourly employees, supervisory and management ranks were exclusively white. Senior managers lived in larger houses in the "better" sections of town and enjoyed a number of privileges, such as golf and tennis club memberships. Moreover, "You might be able to ring the bell [at school] or you were given something that somebody else felt that they would like . . . because his dad was a little higher on the totem pole," William Bosch recalled. Some who grew up in Benham and Lynch still remember the sting of such distinctions. "We were diverse long before diversity was fashionable," writes Jerry Richardson, who lived in Lynch. "There were Poles, Czechs, Italians, Scots, Africans, and many more. The ethnic distinctions weren't discussed. The real differences were in terms of job descriptions. Was your father a miner or a boss? If he was a boss, what level of boss was he? I have good friends who were scarred by these class distinctions."[18]

Class structure based upon company position ultimately had less impact within the black community than it did in the white community. Most blacks were not permitted to work at anything other than low-level positions. Many white ethnic workers also worked these jobs. And although Jim Crow laws enforced a segregated social structure aboveground, within each town's black community—especially within black schools—there were different status criteria. Rank was determined by one's ability, achievement, and citizenship, not an artificially depressed factor such as job level. The ability to succeed as a result of personal worth was an important element in the communal and educational experiences that shaped the memories and values of those who later became Eastern Kentucky Social Club members.

The stories and memories of Eastern Kentucky Social Club members and others who lived in Benham and Lynch during their youth describe a special moment and place where the social fabric of coal towns was woven into a unique pattern of community life and values. It was not an especially easy time because of the depression, World War II, union-management conflicts, declines in the coal industry, and racism and segregation. Despite such difficulties, however, Benham and Lynch provided a safe harbor where families were neither poor nor rich but secure. Most fathers and mothers were able to provide a stable home for their children, who grew up in a segregated environment but whose parents were generally respected by the companies and white residents for having strong work ethics and family values. Black families received good health services, adequate housing, and, above all, quality educations.

The company towns of Benham and Lynch provided what many communities want but most do not achieve—an environment where young people could come of age immersed in sound values and encouraged to develop a sense of meaning and worth. It is little wonder that those who lived in that time and place should want to celebrate their heritage. The Eastern Kentucky Social Club was founded to enable them to do just that.

CHAPTER 7

❧ ❧ ❧ "One Close Community": The Eastern Kentucky Social Club

The formation of social clubs by immigrant ethnic groups is a well-established feature of the American social landscape. The United States is a nation of migrants, and every major city hosts at least a few such organizations, each dedicated to celebrating the food, drink, music, dance, and lore of a specific heritage. Following World War II, thousands of migrants from the Appalachian mountains streamed north in increasingly larger waves to seek jobs. The Great Migration, as this mass movement came to be called, found urban leaders, social workers, educators, and others in the destination cities struggling to cope with the arrival of so many newcomers. Migrants also struggled to acclimate to a new environment and the new lifestyles found in the cities. Like European and other ethnic groups, they created organizations, usually for social purposes, to affirm their identities, remain connected to their roots, and preserve their heritage.

Many city leaders and professionals, including some from the Appalachian region, did not believe Appalachians could or would form viable organizations. "Nobody ever organized that population" remarked a civic leader in Chicago. An Appalachian migrant leader agreed. "It's like trying to organize a bucket of worms" he said about his efforts to organize migrants in Cleveland.[1] Contrary to these stereotypical views, however, Appalachian migrants did form their own organizations.

Perhaps the earliest Appalachian migrant organization was the West Virginia Society, founded in 1917 by people who had been recruited to Akron to work for the Firestone Tire and Rubber Company, the B. F. Goodrich Company, and the Goodyear Tire and Rubber Company. The purpose of the West Virginia Society was primarily social, and its annual picnics in the 1930s drew more than ten thousand people.[2] Migrants, mainly from Kentucky, established similar organizations during the 1960s in Hamilton, Ohio, and the greater Detroit area. Stan Dezarn founded the O'Tucks group in Hamilton to promote "the music, song, cultural heritage, and the humor that is so prevalent in my Kentucky home . . . the mountain counties." Annual summer picnics attracted hundreds of participants. The Kentuckians of Michigan, formed by migrants who worked in the automobile industry, has held annual picnics since 1960. Member Charles Lowe describes the yearly event, which draws more than a thousand people, as a day "that takes us back home without having to take the trip."[3] Our Common Heritage in Dayton also holds an annual event and other activities designed to "promote awareness of Appalachian culture." Lela Estes, a founder and president of Our Common Heritage, saw the organization grow from a loose network of migrants to an important community organization supporting urban Appalachians and their families.[4]

Not all groups created by urban Appalachians were social in nature. The Urban Appalachian Council (UAC) in Cincinnati grew out of efforts during the 1960s to build an advocacy organization in that city's Appalachian migrant neighborhoods. Since then UAC has promoted Appalachian culture and heritage and served as an advocacy and service organization for migrants and their descendants who live in predominately Appalachian neighborhoods. Cincinnati is also the home of the annual Appalachian Festival sponsored by the Appalachian Community Development Association. The thirty-second annual Appalachian Festival in 2002 drew nearly fifty thousand people to the four-day event.[5] In Chicago, the Council of the Southern Mountains (CSM), with funding from a local businessman and philanthropist, opened an office in 1963. Later named the Chicago Southern Center, the undertaking sought to help migrants adjust to life in the city and prepare them for returning to the mountains. Over its ten years of operation in Uptown, the center's mission shifted toward a human service and cultural pride orientation. The strained relationship between CSM's office in Berea, Kentucky, and leaders in Chicago, however, eventually led to the center closing in 1973.[6]

African American migrants from the Deep South formed similar clubs, albeit for reasons beyond self-help and cultural sustenance. As E. Franklin Frazier notes, "The great significance which 'social' life has for Negroes has been due to their exclusion from participation in American life. The numerous 'social' clubs and other forms of voluntary associations which have existed among them provided a form of participation that compensated for their rejection by the white community."[7] Consequently, a rich associational life grew up among black migrants; it was based around churches, taverns, dance halls, and settlement houses and reinforced by frequent family reunions.[8]

African American migrant social clubs are most often organized around towns or places of origins, for example, the Tunica Club in St. Louis, the Charleston Club in Detroit, and the Greenville Club in Chicago. Originally, the first-generation migrant founders viewed them as settings for mutual aid, exchange of information, and formal and informal socializing. Now they are also a link to the past for the founders' multigenerational descendants, who have growing interest in their southern roots, genealogy, and racial history.[9] Among the groups is the Eastern Kentucky Social Club, which was formed by African American migrants who wanted to maintain long-standing friendships and celebrate a heritage rooted in the coalfields of southeastern Kentucky.

Life immediately after World War II was good for most residents of Benham and Lynch despite postwar pressures and labor strife. But the economic boom in the coalfields of eastern Kentucky was at an end, and the mines began closing. The push-pull economic phenomena that propelled the outward migration of white Appalachians from the end of the 1940s until well into the 1970s had the same effect on the black miners and their families who lived in Harlan County. The increased use of automated machinery meant that more coal could be mined using fewer workers. This had a compound effect on black miners, the least likely to be trained in using new mining methods or given jobs operating the new equipment.

As mines reduced production, automated, or shut down, unemployed African American miners moved their families to industrial centers where economic and social opportunities for workers were more plentiful. Many young people who returned home after military service or one or two years at college found few jobs available, even if they wanted to go into the mines. There was, however, the promise of work and careers in Detroit, Cleveland, Chicago, and other northern cities. Furthermore, many young black men and women in Benham and Lynch were prepared to leave the area. Eddie McDonald's move to Detroit after a year at Knoxville College was typical: "Well, the work, I never wanted to be a coal miner and my father . . . didn't want his children to go in the coal mine. So, in the area where I came from they believed in education, of sending their children to college . . . to make a better life than what was given there at that particular time and the only industry was the coal mine and a lot of us just went to different cities to try to make a living for ourselves." Porter G. Peeples, president of the Urban League in Lexington, Kentucky, was also ready to migrate. "The job opportunities that were there would have been coal mining," he says, "and my father, like many other fathers during the time when I was growing up were pretty adamant that they wanted us to have another opportunity. . . . [mining] was a no-no, you graduate and you go."[10]

Founding members Della and Willie Watts in Cleveland, Ohio. (Authors' collection)

Detroit Chapter President Eddie McDonald and wife Alberta. (Authors' collection)

Willie Watts remembered people taking Greyhound buses out of Harlan, Pineville, or Middlesboro. They would "head up into Cincinnati, coming through Lexington. Some would go out to Louisville and head up [Interstate] 65. That's how Chicago, Detroit, Cleveland, New York became enriched with people from Kentucky." Della Watts concurred, speaking about her family's move to Cleveland in 1955: "Our parents were coal miners, . . . when coal mining started shutting down or going out of business my parents came here. Willie's parents came here also and his sister and myself, we went to school together in Kentucky, so when she moved up to Cleveland . . . we just made contact with one another."[11]

The Founding of the Eastern Kentucky Social Club

The Eastern Kentucky Social Club began in 1967 when seven friends in Cleveland gathered at the home of Armelia Moss to talk about the possibility of a reunion of migrants from Benham and Lynch. The conversation carried over during the next two years at regular gatherings on Cleveland's East Side. "We decided we needed an official place of meeting," remarks Willie Watts. "A friend of ours that went to school with us down in Kentucky, Elmer Chide, had a bar called the Red Satin Lounge, and this is where we started our meetings. We started from the original seven and chose Robert Lee as president."[12]

The group, which included Moss, Della and Willie Watts, Roland Motley, James Meadows, and Clarence and Betty Rodgers, held barbeque dinners, cabaret parties, and raffles to underwrite the costs of the reunion. The first was held on Cleveland's East Side at Shakerlee Hall in 1970. News about plans for the event spread by word of mouth among migrants from Harlan County who lived in Atlanta, Detroit, Chicago, and, of course, in Benham and Lynch. "It was just friends telling friends and families telling families. We sent no invitations for our first reunion, it was just by word of mouth," remembers Della Watts. Gean Austin, longtime president of the Lynch chapter of the EKSC, attended the first reunion. "My brother lived in Cleveland, and he told me about it. He called me, so we decided to drive up. It was hectic, small, cause they had it in a small club." The first reunion drew an unexpectedly large crowd, and the party eventually spilled out into the parking lot. The reunion in Cleveland was so popular that within a year local branches of the club had been formed in Chicago, Detroit, and back home in Lynch to host future gatherings.[13]

Annual Reunions

The second reunion was held in Detroit and the third in Chicago, Willie Watts recalls, "because we had a lot of Kentuckians in Detroit, and I think it was at this time that we started thinking about a Cleveland chapter and Detroit chapter . . . and a Chicago chapter." Ultimately, fourteen chapters were formed in such places as Atlanta, Los Angeles, Hartford, Dayton, Indianapolis, Louisville, Milwaukee, and New York City. Eleven of the chapters were still active in 2003.[14]

EKSC members are not just from Benham and Lynch. At first the organization was called the Southeastern Kentucky Social Club, "sim-

Andrea Massey and Gean Austin in Lynch, Kentucky. (Authors' collection)

ply because we came from the southeastern part of Kentucky, Harlan County," Watts observes. The name was changed to the Eastern Kentucky Social Club because so many others from the area were interested in attending the reunions. Friends and family who lived throughout the region in Pine Mountain, Whitesburg, Jenkins, Cumberland, Hazard, Pikeville, Harlan, Barboursville and Middlesboro, Kentucky, also attend the reunions. "It wasn't just coal mining," Watts adds, "it was church and the church picnics and high school. We played football, basketball and then we had out of school softball . . . we just all became rivals, and when we had a party, they'd come over here or we'd go over there. We would all just get together, and it all came from sports, coal mining, and church, and we still keep those three alive now." Although early documents of the club indicate that members have roots in one of eight Kentucky counties (Bell, Boyd, Clay, Floyd, Harlan, Letcher, Perry, and Pike), most of its activities and active members come from Lynch, Benham, and adjacent communities in Harlan County.[15]

Clearly, the reunions are the essence of the EKSC because they sustain the spirit of the organization and its members. From the beginning, the events were sponsored by a local chapter and now have been held throughout the country. "The first reunion was just hugging and kissing and reminiscing . . . and that's what the EKSC has always been about for the past twenty-eight or twenty-nine years," Willie Watts says. "Our main focus," adds Della Watts, "is just 'Let's stay together.' We do not want to lose our roots where we came from because we are not ashamed of that, and to love and support one another." Andrea Massey, from the Lynch chapter, echoes that sentiment: "The purpose of the EKSC is to keep the families together, keep them coming together." Labor Day weekend was eventually chosen for the annual reunion so families can arrive on Friday night or Saturday, enjoy the festivities, and travel home on Monday.[16] Della Watts describes a typical reunion:

> Usually the first day we get there, a lot of people come in early on Wednesday, Thursday, . . . Friday is registration, usually there is a Friday activity. We've had like a little disco or some kind of get-acquainted thing for that Friday evening, Saturday they have activities for the children during the day, you have a tour, normally a tour through the city. We've had boat rides on Friday evenings and then that Saturday during the day, I'm thinking about what we did in Atlanta, they had a jazz fest for us, we had bingos, a lot of people go to the baseball games. One of the big things . . . in Kentucky is to go to the race track. They do different things depending on what your city is, that's what we highlight in that particular city. Sunday we have church service, and we have communion after church service, and then you have the banquet Sunday night. Like starting on Fridays you have hospitality suites on different floors, and people are just going from place to place. It's just a fun thing.[17]

For Eddie McDonald, the annual gatherings are remarkable events:

> How so many black people can get together, . . . just a jolly, jolly good
> time, we have some renowned speakers in the country to speak at our
> annual banquet which will be held on a Sunday night and to meet old
> friends that you haven't seen in twenty-five and thirty years, people that
> you've gone to school with, people that you played football with, basket-
> ball with and socialize in Kentucky, you see these people, some of the el-
> der people that helped raise you, as that saying goes it takes a village to
> raise a child, and that's what happened in our community, and you see
> these people, and they are happy to be united again, and that is once a
> year and we look forward to doing that once a year.[18]

Merlene Davis, who is married to a member, has described the EKSC
as a club "united by a region and a sense of family." She joined 1,800
eastern Kentucky migrants and family members at the reunion in Dayton in 2000. In a story for the *Lexington Herald-Leader,* she recorded
"gleeful shouts of joy, the tight embraces, and the shared memories.
Walking from one place to another was extremely time-consuming.
With each three or four steps, another old friend was spotted, and love
had to be exchanged. No one rushed. It was a once-a-year experience.
Former high school ballplayers sought out teammates; first cousins
searched for second cousins; New Yorkers looked for Californians."[19]
Ruth Davis, whose coal miner father was forced to move to Cleveland
when the mine in which he worked closed, was a part of a joyful throng
in a Cleveland hotel lobby during the 1994 reunion. "This is something
we can all be proud of," she maintains. "It's our way of remembering."[20]

Memorial Day Homecomings

While the annual Labor Day reunions are held in cities across the country, the Memorial Day weekend is a time to go home. Memorial Day
homecoming in Benham, Lynch, and surrounding towns such as Cumberland, Evarts, and Totz is an intergral part of EKSC activities. The
Lynch chapter normally plans activities for the weekend. As Andrea
Massey describes the event:

> We usually start out on Friday night. Well, this past year [1997] we had a
> Pirate Celebration, the school was the Lynch Pirates. Saturday picnick-

ing and then Saturday was the dance, and on Sunday we had a memorial service for the deceased. Sunday night we have the last function, which is the dance here at the school [EKSC Hall]. . . . I think Memorial Day weekend . . . is just like a little reunion leading up to the big reunion, and plus they get to visit their families. It is the memorial time for us here so everybody comes home. They've got to come back to Lynch.[21]

"These are my people, my roots," remarks William Jackson, a sergeant in the Los Angeles County Sheriff's Department, who returned to Lynch for the 1991 Memorial Day weekend. "I come back and walk up and down these streets, and I'm home." Porter G. Peeples has described the weekend "as almost like a small Mardi Gras . . . because people are just walking about and socializing. One would think that if you do this every year, Memorial Day, Labor Day, that it would have gotten old, but there is still just as much exuberance and happiness and warm fondness for seeing and greeting one another again, and it is so obvious."[22]

Throughout the year, EKSC local chapters hold monthly meetings and fund-raisers to prepare for the next year's events. The California chapter's Web-site and the "Eastern Kentucky Social Club's Biography" prepared by Andrea Massey detail these activities. Several events are scheduled each year to raise funds to help with travel costs associated with attending annual reunions and support key African American organizations and causes. The Detroit chapter has contributed each year to the NAACP, the Sickle Cell Anemia Foundation, and the Negro Fund Dinner. Funds from the Lynch chapter have supported contributions to the Kentucky State Police Christmas Fund, student field trips at several local schools, and two annual scholarships for minority students.[23]

The EKSC held its thirty-third reunion in Louisville, Kentucky in 2002, and the 2003 and 2004 events were scheduled for Atlanta and Las Vegas. Although the club remains very active, the question of the group's future is of growing importance. It is an issue that gnaws at the founders and other long-term members. "At our workshops, one thing we're working on is to recruit young people from our grandchildren and our children. To keep this legacy going," observes Della Watts. "My children, I doubt very seriously, would have as much interest as some of the young people that have graduated from Benham and Lynch. Now I think they will be the ones that will keep this legacy going." Gean Austin is also concerned about the future of the EKSC. "Well, basically, I don't hold much future for it," he says. "Because now as the older people pass away, the younger ones are really not interested in this heritage. Even though they come every year on Memorial Day to enjoy the festivities, they are not interested in it [the EKSC], so I don't see much of a future for it."[24]

It is difficult, however, to overlook the group's sustained and lasting impact. For more than thirty years a large contingent of friends and acquaintances from throughout the United States has gathered annually to celebrate their friendships and their roots in a small valley and a few surrounding towns in the Appalachian mountains. Many of them left the mountains when they were youngsters, but each year they are bound together by Appalachian ties of a common experience and ingrained values shaped by a special time and place.

The opportunities, security, relative simplicity, and closeness of life in the black communities of model coal towns gave residents a positive feeling about Benham and Lynch that did not diminish after migration. In the words of one commentator on black miners' experiences in the Appalachian coalfields, "Their contributions in building community were as significant as the tons of coal they produced."[25] Given the tempo, complexity, and racial tensions of the urban settings in which they arrived, nostalgia for the coalfields may have been intensified. These experiences are reflected in the Eastern Kentucky Social Club because members share a history that was, overall, a positive experience. Although many commentators accurately depict life in the coal towns of Appalachia as demeaning, dangerous, paternalistic, and exploitative, that is not the perspective of EKSC members. They are vitally aware of the hardships that black coal miners experienced and do not gloss over them by any means. They do, however, acknowledge the positive aspects of the lives that they and their families had in the Appalachian coalfields. For them, the Eastern Kentucky Social Club is "one close community" that still celebrates those experiences.

CHAPTER 8

❦ ❦ ❦ "They Love Coming Home":
Appalachian Ties That Bind

> When I needed it, the old place of my boyhood
> would yet be there waiting for me with all its
> wisdom and purpose, if not in stone and wood
> and iron, then still in my memory and my heart.
> —Homer Hickam Jr., *Sky of Stone*

In the end it is fair to ask, What is unusual about the Eastern Kentucky Social Club? Overall, its members do not seem exceptional in comparison to other members of African American or Appalachian migrant organizations, to other black miners, or even to other black residents of company-owned towns in the Appalachian coalfields. In fact, there appear to be, at some levels, more similarities than differences among these groups.[1]

African American migrants from the Deep South have established many urban associations that are rooted in communities that often experienced much more devastating forms of racism than those found in southeastern Kentucky. The EKSC is one of many such African American voluntary organizations, and its existence is not an unusual phenomenon. Other Appalachian migrants have also formed organizations and social clubs. West Virginians were extensively organized in Akron, Ohio, well before World War II. Other Appalachian clubs, service organizations, and advocacy groups began forming in the 1960s and 1970s in cities such as Chicago, Detroit, Cleveland, Dayton, and Cincinnati. The EKSC, then, can be seen as just another Appalachian organization among several that formed after the Great Appalachian Migration of the 1940s and 1950s.

Moreover, there were black miners in the United States for decades before the Kentucky coalfields opened, and their working conditions were hazardous and harsh. Historically, social conditions were especially brutal for black miners in Alabama, whereas West Virginia coalfields provided a comparatively more progressive social atmosphere. In that context, Harlan County was not the first, the worst, or necessarily the best place for black miners and their families to live and work.

Finally, Benham and Lynch were constructed more than thirty years after the model town movement began in America; the philosophical underpinnings of welfare capitalism were fairly well developed by the time they were applied in southeastern Kentucky. Standard industrial practices of that era governed the construction and operation of such towns. Although considered state-of-the-art at the time, they can also be considered as typical examples of model towns owned by major coal corporations during the early twentieth century. In fact, towns of this type were not unique to the Appalachian coalfields. Similar industrial towns were found on the economic landscape throughout Europe and North America during this era.

We do not argue that the Eastern Kentucky Social Club is exceptional; its members and their history clearly share many characteristics with comparable social groups. Nevertheless, a close examination of the historical record and collective memory of EKSC members does produce a distinctive perspective.

The Eastern Kentucky Social Club has much in common with other urban black social clubs across the nation. What sets it apart are its members' roots in the Appalachian coalfields and coal towns of Harlan County. Members of the EKSC lived and worked alongside European immigrants and native white mountaineers. They participated in the formation of labor unions and had relatively good pay, decent housing, and educational opportunities of quality. None of these are typical experiences of the many other African American social club members who migrated from the Deep South, where they lived in rural poverty, often as sharecroppers.

Generally, the groups that white Appalachian migrants formed were not the usual self-help organizations composed by other, particularly foreign-born, immigrant groups. Nor have white Appalachian migrant associations been as influential in urban communities, especially in politics, as many black and European migrant groups have been.[2] Perhaps that is because of the degree of importance that unions have played in the lives of migrants from coalfields. Unions were strong advocates for their members, provided access to health care and a number of social services, and took a major role in local politics. For the most part, unionized urban Appalachian workers, both black and white, did not need self-help or political advocacy organizations because such things were taken care of. What many migrants did need, however, was a means to socialize with "their own kind" and a way to connect with their mountain homes. Consequently, they often formed social clubs like the EKSC.[3]

Some characteristics of the Eastern Kentucky Social Club are typical of Appalachian migrant organizations, whereas others are unique. The EKSC is typical in the sense that migrants nearly always seek out each other for support and to maintain links with their geographic and cultural origins. EKSC members have indeed formed a social network to preserve fond memories and relationships over time and distance. Yet several additional characteristics set the group apart from other Appalachian migrant organizations. Its members are all African American rather than predominantly Caucasian; it is a national organization, with active chapters in eleven cities rather than being based principally in a single metropolitan area; and a substantial majority of its members are migrants or their descendants whose roots are in communities located within a few miles of each other in southeastern Kentucky.

Moreover, African American religious congregations both in the mountains and in the cities have traditionally played an important role in addressing not only the spiritual but also the political and economic issues their members face. This contrasts with the churches favored by white Appalachian migrants, which generally avoid political entanglements or large-scale social welfare initiatives. Many white Appalachians in the Great Migration brought their union backgrounds with them. In the same era, migrants who formed the Eastern Kentucky Social Club often were union members and members of socially active black churches.

The story of the Eastern Kentucky Social Club, although not unique, nevertheless fills a gap in understanding black miners in Appalachia.

Most literature on that region focuses on blacks in the coalfields of West Virginia and Alabama. John Henever gives only passing mention to blacks in his momentous account of the union organizing struggles in Harlan County. Shaunna Scott, a sociologist who wrote a thorough-going analysis of class consciousness in the county, expresses regret in her epilogue that she was unable to include African American families in the study. G. C. Jones's first-person narrative *Growing Up Hard in Harlan County* gives no hint of the thousands of black miners and their families who lived along Looney Creek. And Barbara Freese, in her wide-ranging narrative *Coal: A Human History,* fails to mention either Kentucky or African Americans.[4]

Thus, the EKSC membership's historical experience in the model coal towns along the banks of Looney Creek presents an important dimension of the African American experience in the Kentucky coal-fields, albeit one not available to many other black miners and their families. Indeed, the distinctiveness of that experience is the basis of the club. The history of the EKSC gives a particular voice to the role of African Americans in Kentucky's economy, culture, politics, and labor relations.

At this point it is important to recall the evolution from early "coal camps" to the later "model" coal towns and recognize the distinctions between them. It is all too easy to assume that all coal towns were alike and gave their residents similar experiences. Janet Greene, Robert Munn, and others are clear about the contrasts between "camps" and the "model" towns in their writing about coal towns and their resi-dents.[5]

The original coal camps were often the fiefdoms of individual mine owners, offering little more than a job and a roof over a miner's head. Early mines typically were small, independent operations owned by an overweening and authoritative "coal baron" who saw the camp as a bare necessity and not something worth a substantial investment of re-sources. These often undercapitalized endeavors frequently meant unsafe working environments in the mines and equally poor living con-ditions aboveground. Even within this period, though, some coal towns were better than others. Coalwood, West Virginia, for example, as de-scribed by novelist Homer Hickam, was founded in 1887 by George L.

Carter, who "wanted his miners to have a decent place to live." Moreover, Coalwood had parks, sidewalks, and a good water source—conditions that raised its standard of living.

The patterns of individual mine ownership began to change around 1900 when major corporations such as U.S. Steel, Consolidated Coal, the Island Creek Coal Company, Inland Steel, and International Harvester began to play a larger role in coalfields. As these well-financed companies developed extensive mining operations across the central Appalachian coalfields, some invested in "model" communities for their workers. Building a town that had a suitable municipal infrastructure, housing, recreational and health facilities, and good schools was a competitive necessity, or "good business," in accord with the principles of welfare capitalism.[6] Providing for the comfort and contentment of workers in a closely supervised community, however, was also a means of exerting control over workers and their families. It was this "proposition" that George Carter talked about when building Coalwood. Families there lived in reasonably good conditions but understood the rules and only "got along by going along."

A rough chronological pattern emerges in the development of these communities. In the early stages (1880–1900), mining camps were generally austere places; many of the lasting images that the public holds about life in coal towns come from this time. Other developments, such as the construction of model coal towns, occurred during the Progressive Era, or between 1900 and 1920. A period of slow decline began during the late 1920s, accelerated in the 1930s, and continued until most company towns were sold off after World War II. These are, of course, not mutually exclusive temporal categories. Differences emerged over time and involved a large degree of overlap, but these temporal distinctions are helpful in interpreting the historical evolution that occurred in the coalfields.

Within that context, Kentucky's small number of model coal towns played an important role in developing practices that still prevail in contemporary corporate employee relations policies. In particular, International Harvester's and U.S. Steel's model towns constitute significant examples of industrial urban design that have largely gone unnoticed in the history of planning. Many studies of coal towns are available in the literature on Appalachia. At most, however, they are only briefly noted in the literature of city planning, which focuses heavily on experiments in metropolitan areas, such as Pullman in the Chicago area. Nonetheless, Benham and Lynch were important elements of a corporate effort to create controlled physical and social environments that continued to evolve throughout the rest of the twentieth century.

Benham and Lynch were not only model towns of their day but also working prototypes for the future. A striking example is the Toyota automobile plant in Scott County, Kentucky. Upon opening in 1985, it attracted white and black migrants from other American regions, principally the South and Appalachia. Toyota spent $20 million to build and improve local schools and later built a company-sponsored recreation and fitness center for employees. The corporation provides the usual array of worker benefits, operates a small company store, sponsors employee contests and sports teams, influences local and state politics and policies, uses philanthropy to project a benevolent image, and employs all those strategies to resist unionization. Perhaps most telling is Toyota's corporate endeavor to define itself and its workers as one "family," as evidenced on its Web-site. These characteristics are strikingly similar to those found in the Appalachian hometowns of the EKSC membership. Clearly, EKSC members were important participants in an evolutionary process of corporate social and physical planning that can be traced from Harlan County in the early twentieth century to Scott County in Kentucky in the early twenty-first century.

Building Up Steam on the "Aboveground Railroad"

With this information in mind, we can again ask, Why, then, is the Eastern Kentucky Social Club important? Why are EKSC members so cohesive, and why do they hold their roots in "Bloody Harlan" in such a positive light? We believe that the importance of the EKSC lies both in its place in the history of Appalachia and its place in the lives of its members. Three general themes emerge from interviews with club members and the historical record of blacks in southeastern Kentucky coalfields: ambiguity, opportunity and achievement, and race relations.

Ambiguity

In the early-twentieth-century coalfields of southeastern Kentucky there is ample evidence of exploitation and benevolence, segregation and integration, company paternalism and worker independence, and racism and acceptance. Model towns of the Appalachian coalfields like Benham and Lynch were neither heaven nor hell for EKSC members and their predecessors. Yet for black miners and their families, the towns were influential stops along a path that led from slavery to success. Although most EKSC members would indeed define themselves as successful, their story is not one of living the American dream as much as living the African American reality. Perhaps their sense of success, made evident in their interviews, is precisely what prevents them from emphasizing the hardships of life and labor in Appalachian coalfields, much less the harsh racial realities of the Upland South during the early twentieth century. They see their experiences in Benham and Lynch as a part of a pattern of progress and, ultimately, achievement. In this flow of events, negative aspects tend to be downplayed or overlooked altogether, yet the underlying ambiguity of their circumstance remains clear.

Opportunity and Achievement

Benham and Lynch play a significant role in any understanding of the Eastern Kentucky Social Club because life in those model coal towns marked a turning point in the history of club members and their forebears. If anything, working for International Harvester and U.S. Steel offered opportunity and a chance for achievement. The towns' important role in the formation of industrial policies and employee-employer relations continues to endure in the American workplace.

The historical importance of Lynch and Benham to the Eastern Kentucky Social Club is matched by their significance in the history of urban planning and industrial policy development. Many families in the club participated in a postbellum Aboveground Railroad through which emancipated blacks from the plantation South moved into the Appalachian coalfields for a generation or two and then into urban and industrial America. Their history shows that they were not passive subjects of economic and social conditions but employed the active tactics of production control, labor mobility, unionization, alliance with national civil rights organizations, and, ultimately, migration to control their own destinies. To gain the greatest social benefit, they combined these coalfield stratagems with the benefits of living in a model town: decent housing and public health, opportunity for a good education, close-knit families and communities, practical industrial skills, and regular wages.

Harlan County's miners, both black and white, saw an opportunity and took it. It was in the model coal towns of Harlan County that Eastern Kentucky Social Club members' Aboveground Railroad built up a head of steam. The social benefits they found and used in Benham and Lynch in particular provided momentum to carry them into successful urban industrial and professional careers.

Negotiating Racial Situations

Race is an overarching presence throughout this narrative, tempering the notion of "success" every step of the way. Memphis Tennessee Garrison, for instance, makes clear that blacks in the coalfields had to constantly negotiate the politics of family and community "situations," labor "situations," and racial "situations."[7] Within the obvious constraints of segregation, many EKSC members managed to take advantage of Appalachia's golden age of coal mining. Some even basked in its afterglow during the period of decline, but they did it at a price. "Going along to get along," for example, meant living under Jim Crow aboveground while being remanded underground to manual work with little hope of promotion to machine operator or management positions.

It is important not to judge racial conditions of the early twentieth century through the still-flawed yet clearer lenses of the early twenty-first. Although the equivocal attitudes that Harvester officials displayed toward building the "Negro" YMCA in Benham were appalling, for example, they were usual for that time and place. This does not justify the underlying racism and paternalism inherent in the construction of the facility, but it does provide insight on the ambiguous social situations that black miners and their families learned to negotiate in the coalfields. Although companies took great public relations credit for model towns, theirs was a begrudging munificence, especially where black workers were concerned.

Nevertheless, most current EKSC members left the coalfields with at least a sound high school education, a strong work ethic, close family ties, a pragmatic approach to race relations, and a positive attitude toward their communities of origin. These characteristics, derived directly or indirectly from their experiences growing up and working in model company towns, create a binding tie despite the members' diaspora.

The ongoing viability of the Eastern Kentucky Social Club is not assured. Perhaps the greatest threat to the organization today is the one that many similar migrant or ethnic organizations have faced: aging membership. As the second, third, and fourth generations spread out into urban American society, there is less interest in the organization. Many similar associations have disappeared or continue to struggle along, dependent upon a small core of aging leaders. Whether the EKSC can continue as a viable organization is unknown, but one role it may play in the future is to sustain the heritage of a new generation of African Americans who are increasingly interested in their genealogy and history. For the present, however, it continues to play a lively and integral part in the lives of a generation of migrants from Harlan County, Kentucky.

The sense of place and love for the mountains and coal towns of Appalachia, expressed by Effie Waller Smith in her poems and Homer Hickam in his novels, is demonstrated in the spirit of the Eastern Kentucky Social Club. Andrea Massey may have put it best: "If I was ending a book, or writing a book about the EKSC, I would say that it has been a club that was formed to keep people together, to meet every year. It has been wonderful years for us now. We've been to several different cities. We should always try to stay together. You would find that these are some of the best people from eastern Kentucky and, at all times, they come home. They love coming home!"[8]

Afterword:
Values, Spoken and Unspoken

William H. Turner

"What did you think of this fighter?" heavyweight boxing champion Joe Louis was asked at the end of his famous bout against Max Schmeling in front of seventy thousand fans at Yankee Stadium in 1938. Joe, known as the Brown Bomber, replied in his own unique way: "I ain't nevah hit nobody dat hard, dat many times and he didn't go down. If he hadnt'a fell after I hit him with dat las' uppercut, I was gonna go 'round back a' him, to see jes' what wuz holdin' him up!"[1]

In the late 1930s it could be accurately declared that African American miners and migrants in the coal camps of Harlan County, Kentucky—in Benham, Black Mountain, Cumberland, Evarts, Harlan, and Lynch—had much in common with Joe Louis. They, too, were fighters. Louis was then the heavyweight champion of the world (which meant he was the greatest man in the world). The African American miners and migrants described by Tom Wagner and Phil Obermiller were workers and residents—fighting to maintain jobs and their human dignity—in a region where the vast majority of people was often misunderstood and victimized by exploitation from the outsiders who controlled the coal business in corporate-owned coal towns. They were workers, fighters in an unpredictable industry, an enterprise that made many outsiders wealthy but more often than not rendered residents victims of long-term economic distress and dislocation. Even so, the African American miners and migrants discussed and heard from in this book lived and worked in some of the world's most productive coalfields and in some of its greatest coal towns.

By the time the Brown Bomber pounded the Aryan celebrity, knocking him to the canvas three times, thousands of coal miners had lived in Lynch, Kentucky, for almost half a century. And although their highly capitalized coal town was isolated from the main currents of American life and culture, it was among the most self-contained and prosperous coal camps in the world. Lynch rightfully claimed as its own "the largest coal tipple in the world." Who could tell those who lived in Lynch that it was not the greatest coal camp in the world or that they were not a special breed of people—a great people—among the people of the earth?

But in the words of Langston Hughes, one of Joe Louis's contemporaries, life for African American miners and migrants in the coal camps of Kentucky was "no crystal stair." They were hit many times by the bust-and-boom cycle of the coal industry. They clashed with social and economic forces that were unique and distinctive perhaps only to Appalachia. More often than most other Americans—red, white, or yellow—or their fellow black citizens elsewhere, blacks in Appalachian coal camps, places most of their fellow citizens had never heard of, endured and triumphed over the hits on them. The title of James Baldwin's book about black southern migrants to Harlem, *Nobody Knows My Name,* was evocative and representational of that life then. Nobody knew the names of the subjects of this book, and few recognized the names of where they lived. Even now, at the dawn of the twenty-first century when Appalachian coal towns such as Lynch are but remnants of their former selves, today's generation, the offspring and descendants of African American miners and migrants, still live virtually invisible lives. Appalachia is still perceived as a region where one does not expect to find people of African descent.[2]

Starting there—when looked at as members of a detested racial minority who came to live amid a subpopulation who themselves were beyond the pale of the white American mainstream—the first blows were struck in the fight waged by blacks in Appalachia's coal camps. That battle in and of itself was special. In the coal mines of Harlan County, Kentucky, the stereotypical black southerner (Sambo) met the matchless and hapless white Appalachian (Lil' Abner)—also pigeonholed in the fabrications and myths concocted by scholars, researchers, and varied media types over the years. That had to make for some spellbinding scenarios for blacks who went to work in the mines and sought to hew lives of hope from beneath the mountains of despair that enclosed eastern Kentucky's coal miners and their progeny. Like a collective John Henry—the Steel Driving Man—black coal miners surely had to exhibit enormous patience, persistence, perspective, and pride, all of which are evident in the stories told in this book.[3]

Like Joe Louis's challenger, they were hit harder than most. Men made their livings in deep, dank, and dark places and in situations that most other Americans cannot imagine. Wagner and Obermiller, after looking at the general history of coal mining in central Appalachia and the back-breaking work commonly associated with it (not to mention the particularly tough social times experienced by black miners and their families), could easily have turned the question put to Louis and asked black coal-mining families, "What kept you standing, what was behind you, why didn't you fall, what was holding you up?"

When the first wave of black men—my grandfather's generation—

Removing top in the Lynch mine.

went into the central Appalachian coal mines three decades before the Great Depression, it was common for a thousand or more of them to die within a year, mostly as a result of regularly occurring cave-ins and explosions caused by methane gas and the fine dust that permeated the pits.

Like Joe Louis's adversary, African American miners and migrants didn't fall, at least not easily, not until after a hearty fight. Ringed in like Schmeling, the first wave of Alabama-born black coal miners in Kentucky had "nowhere else to go." It's worth noting that the vast majority of the first generation of blacks who migrated to the coalfields of Kentucky just after Joe Louis was born in 1914 came from the same general regions of east central, central, and northeastern Alabama as did Louis, who was born in Chambers County. Their parents, like Louis's, were sharecroppers from the time immediately after slavery until the Great Exodus from the Cotton Belt South, which, beginning in the last decade of the 1800s, took millions of blacks out of the region. Some went to work in the sawmills in the pine woods of Alabama's uplands. America's North Central heartland, primarily cities along the Great Lakes and in the Midwest (Chicago, Cincinnati, Cleveland, Columbus, Detroit, Gary, Indianapolis, and Milwaukee), became home to many blacks making their way out of Dixie.

The flight of other black Alabamians' from the life of poor and exploited rural peasants to that of the urban industrial working class led them to Birmingham, Bessemer, and Fairfield, where they worked in the steel mills. The United States Coal and Coke Company was a dominant force in central Alabama and continued to attract black workers when it opened mines in southeastern Kentucky. The Pittsburgh, Pennsylvania–based company, a subsidiary of the United States Steel Corporation, owned vast coal rights in much of Harlan County, where it built Lynch. By World War II there were more black residents in Lynch than most towns in Kentucky, and a higher percentage of its population was African American than Lexington's.

As Joe Louis put it famously when he defeated Billy Conn in the final seconds of their fight in 1942, "You can run, but you can't hide." Such were the conditions under which black miners and their families lived when they arrived in the coal camps. Chapters 2 and 3 in this volume make the case very well. The total grip that coal companies had on the lives of their employees was made famous in Tennessee Ernie Ford's 1955 hit "Sixteen Tons," written nearly a decade earlier by Merle Travis, whose father and brothers were coal miners in Kentucky. Carl Sandburg echoed these pervasive controls in his poem "The Company Town," which concludes, snappishly, "The company preacher teaches us / what the company thinks is right."[4]

Clearly, the bonds—the ties that bind the subjects of this book in solidarity—were made under the extraordinary conditions typical of Appalachian coal towns developed in the first decades of the twentieth century. The conditions that existed were what Tom Wagner and Phil Obermiller correctly call "a closed economic system. . . . [that was] carefully designed." Although concepts such as "social engineering" and "planned" and "gated" communities have only recently come into the common vocabulary, company towns like Benham, Black Mountain, Evarts, and Lynch were, more than a century ago, "feudal proprietorships that allowed no input on key decisions from a majority of the residents." Many black men who ended up in these coal towns were already prepared to be central parts of the labor machinery that built tipples at the end of hollows. The tons of coal dumped into those tipples came from deep inside the mines, where blacks did much of the backbreaking labor.

For most of the twentieth century and after working underground, side by side with their white counterparts—most of whom in the first wave were of ethnic European origin—black miners took leave to *their* communities on *their* side of the coal camps. They went to company-owned houses where *their* hearts were and where they made *their* big families, worshiped in *their* churches, were educated in *their* schools, partied in *their* juke joints to *their* music, and created *their* own clubs and organizations—*their* Masonic lodges and women's' auxiliaries, sports clubs, and scout troops. Those who didn't migrate were laid to rest in *their* black sections of company-owned graveyards. Such are the ties that bind as voiced by those the authors interviewed, who responded so eloquently and so powerfully.

Dorothy Morrow referred to a man named Limehouse who transported many Alabamians of Joe Louis's generation to Harlan County

Benham Morgan Masonic Lodge, photographed in front of the Rising Star Baptist Church.

for the express purpose of being coal miners. The name *Limehouse*, the only one by which this efficient labor agent was called, is likely a variation on a north Alabama county, Limestone, of which Athens, not far west of Scottsboro and Decatur, is the county seat. The Alabama origins of Harlan County blacks can be seen in death documents I have for more than three hundred blacks who died there between 1950 and 1990. The county of origin listed for "coloreds" in the U.S. Census for 1920 and 1930 confirms these obituary papers.[5] Of course, the "home" chapter of the Eastern Kentucky Social Club is in Harlan County, in Lynch, housed at the venerable old Lynch Colored School. Members of that chapter live in nearby Bell (Middlesboro), Letcher (Jenkins), Perry (Hazard), and Knott (Wheelwright) counties—all within a fifty-mile radius of each other as the crow flies.

When machines replaced strong black arms and backs to get the coal, black miners—the last hired—were more often than not the first fired. "Our daddy got laid-off; I don't know where to, but we're moving!" How often I heard that between 1954, when I was eight, and 1964, when I was eighteen. The heartbreaking, often-repeated scene of an entire family stealing off in the dead of night, all their "stuff" crammed into a rickety old truck, migrating, escaping in a way from the debts owed the company store and going to Chicago, is fresh in my mind.

It is reminiscent of what happened to Joe Louis at the twilight of his great career. Although the Brown Bomber earned close to $5 million

William H. Turner with his siblings. "Y'all's Mama had a baby every nine months and thirty minutes," coal miner William Earl Turner used to tell his children of Naomi ("Punkin") Randolph Turner, whom he married in Lynch, Kentucky, in 1939 when she was fifteen. Among the siblings, left to right, are Barbara Ruth, Marie Antoinette, Irvin Rudolph, Evelyn Ernestine, and William Hobert. Earl and Naomi had three more boys: Mark Anthony, Karl Darnell, and Jeffrey Gene. They also raised Frederick Randolph and Richard Earl—sons of Barbara and Marie. In addition, Naomi Turner began to care for four additional children in 1957 after their mother died. (William H. Turner Collection)

in his career, his money went like the three-minute rounds he boxed. Many black miners, unlike Louis, never earned enough to be extravagant, but neither did most have any savings to speak of. Like Joe, they were generous to each other almost to a fault. Just as the IRS expediently forgot that Joe gave money from several of his fights to the cause of the war and exacted more than $1.2 million from him in back taxes, black miners displaced after decades of toil for "The Company" suffered the mortification and humiliation of having to "get up and go" at a moment's notice. As the authors point out, living in the company's house was contingent on holding one of the company's jobs—clearly, the only game in town. No job? No house! No welcome! At least Joe Louis could repay his debts and support his stays in hospitals for cocaine addiction and paranoia. He bacame, for example, an "official greeter" at Caesar's Palace in Las Vegas. By contrast, the black mining migrants had No patron! No ticket! No token!

Of all the values, spoken and unspoken, that compose the interwoven ties that bind these African American miners and migrants, none are more well regarded than religious beliefs and practices. As a hymn that marked many lives goes, "Bless be the ties that bind, our hearts in Christian love." Religious faith and spirituality run deep—like a seam of coal—among coal-camp blacks. They, in the words of another popular sacred song from the black church, were "going up the rough side of the mountain."[6]

Now, when I go to Atlanta, Chicago, Cleveland, Dayton, Detroit, Hartford, Indianapolis, Louisville, Los Angeles, Lynch, Milwaukee, or New York City (all of which have chapters of the Eastern Kentucky Social Club), I can easily find friends, my Black Mountain "homies," who are at the ends of their migrations from the eastern Kentucky towns of Benham, Cumberland, Evarts, Harlan, and Lynch next to Black Mountain, Kentucky's highest peak in the Appalachian chain. From my research, I know that an extraordinarily high number of migrants during my baby boom generation, and the one just before us, did as Joe Louis did. They served in the U.S. military and used that experience to leverage successful careers.

At the other end of their journey out of coal country, a critical mass of these black miners' and migrants' children moved to the place to which Joe Louis went from Alabama—Detroit. They are like Eddie McDonald, whose interview appears in this book. Eddie's family still runs back and forth between its Alabama origins in Tuskegee, where his grandparents were born and raised and from which they migrated to Benham in the 1920s; to the old home places in Benham on Memorial Day to "decorate the graves" of the grandparents; and to their new homes in Indianapolis, Dayton, and Detroit, where members of the extended McDonald family live now. Although coal mining as they knew it has disappeared from Harlan County, most have taken the values they learned and the communal life they lived there to other places, affecting and transmitting that lifestyle far removed from coal camps.

I encourage readers to make a trip to Harlan County, Kentucky, on Memorial Day weekend or to attend an annual reunion of the Eastern Kentucky Social Club. You will be blessed by a whirlwind of spiritual uplift in being around those who transformed trials and tragedies into triumphs. Joe Louis was called a "credit to his race." As sportswriter Jimmy Cannon responded, "Yes, Louis is a credit to his race—the human race." The true Brown Bombers are the African American miners and migrants described in this book. They, too, are a credit to the human race.

Notes

Introduction

1. Deskins and Kovach, *Effie Waller Smith*, 3–23.

2. Although Benham and Lynch were constructed and managed by subsidiaries, for ease of discussion we will use the parent corporations, International Harvester and U.S. Steel, throughout this volume when referring to the two companies.

3. Stuckert, "Racial Violence in Southern Appalachia," 35–41.

Chapter 1: "Coming Up on the Rough Side of the Mountain"

1. The quotation in the chapter title is from the traditional gospel song "I'm Coming Up on the Rough Side of the Mountain," popularized in the early 1980s by the Rev. F. C. Barnes and the Rev. Janice Brown in an album of the same name. Turner and Cabbell, "Introduction," xviii. The neologism "Afralachian" has recently come into vogue to refer to blacks in Appalachia. See Morgan, "A Way with Words." Although the term enjoys currency among some, Eastern Kentucky Social Club members do not it use in discussing themselves, and we follow their convention in this volume.

2. Woodson, "The Negroes of Cincinnati."

3. Dunaway, *Slavery in the American South*.

4. Inscoe, "Mountain Masters," 123; see also Pudup, "Social Class and Economic Development."

5. Woodson, "The Negroes of Cincinnati"; Inscoe, "Mountain Masters," 126.

6. Stuckert, "Racial Violence in Southern Appalachia," 39; see also Bickley and Ewen, eds., *Memphis Tennessee Garrison*.

7. McKinney, "Southern Mountain Republicans," 493.

8. Quoted in Alexander, "Great Migrations," 62.

9. Trotter, *Coal, Class, and Color*, 46.

10. Sullivan, *Coal Men and Coal Towns*, 186; see also Fishback, "The Miner's Work Environment."

11. Alexander, "Great Migrations," 39.

12. Bickley and Ewen, eds., *Memphis Tennessee Garrison*, 90.

13. Trotter, "Race, Class, and Industrial Change," 63.

14. Turner, "Between Berea (1904) and Birmingham (1908)," 15.

15. Eller, *Miners, Millhands, and Mountaineers*, 168–69; see also Inscoe, "Mountain Masters."

16. Stuckert, "Racial Violence in Southern Appalachia," 39.

17. Turner, "Between Berea (1904) and Birmingham (1908)," 16.

18. Fishback, "The Miner's Work Environment"; Goode, "Introduction to Coal Camp Database"; Sullivan, *Coal Men and Coal Towns*.

19. Shifflett, "What Were Coal Towns Really Like?" 24; Lewis, *Black Coal Miners*, 146.

20. Lewis, *Black Coal Miners*, 146; see also Crawford, *Building the Workingman's Paradise*.

21. Greene, "Strategies for Survival"; Fishback, "The Miner's Work Environment"; Salstrom, *Appalachia's Path*.

22. Munn, "The Development of Model Towns," 244.

23. Sullivan, *Coal Men and Coal Towns*," 161.

24. Ibid., 163

25. Hickam, *Sky of Stone*, 2.

26. Greene, "Strategies for Survival," 41.

27. Bickley and Ewen, eds., *Memphis Tennessee Garrison*, 106.

28. Kelemen "A History of Lynch," 173–75.

29. Hickam, *Sky of Stone*, 106.

30. C. F. Biggert to Alexander Legge, May 23, 1923.

31. Crawford, *Building the Workingman's Paradise*, 7.

32. Bickley and Ewen, eds., *Memphis Tennessee Garrison*, 128.

Chapter 2: "Life for Me Ain't Been No Crystal Stair"

1. The quotation in the chapter title is from the poem "Mother to Son" by Langston Hughes (Rampersad and Rossell, eds., *Poems of Langston Hughes*, 30). Eller, *Miners, Millhands, and Mountaineers*, 169.

2. Trotter, "Race, Class, and Industrial Change," 52.

3. Lewis, *Black Coal Miners*, 127.

4. Interview with Johnnie Jones.

5. Lewis, *Black Coal Miners*, 127.

6. William Bosch to Thomas Wagner, May 31, 2003.

7. Interview with James Hannah.

8. Quoted in Trotter, "Black Miners," 283.

9. Interview with Johnnie Jones.

10. Bickley and Ewen, eds., *Memphis Tennessee Garrison*, 91.

11. Banks, "Coal Miners and Firebrick Workers," 94.

12. Trotter, "Black Miners," 270.

13. Shifflett, "What Were Coal Towns Really Like?" 24.

14. Greene, "Strategies for Survival," 49.

15. Interview with Anlis Lee.

16. Tadlock, "Coal Camps and Character," 21.

17. Fishback, "The Miner's Work Environment," 215, 216.

18. Bickley and Ewen, eds., *Memphis Tennessee Garrison*, 94.

19. Fishback, "The Miner's Work Environment," 214.

20. Ibid., 211.

21. Benham Superintendent R. A. Walter to B. W. Batchelder. April 19, 1920.

22. Ibid.

23. B. W. Batchelder to R. A. Walter, May 24, 1921.

24. Interview with Johnnie Jones.

25. Greene, "Strategies for Survival," 48.

26. Campbell, "Coal Towns," 53.

27. R. A. Walter to B. W. Batchelder, March 8. 1921.

28. Kelemen, "A History of Lynch," 165–66.

29. Interview with Woolford Griffey.

30. Fishback, "The Miner's Work Environment," 220.

31. Interview with Anlis Lee.

32. Fishback, "The Miner's Work Environment," 221.

33. Ibid., 223–24.

34. Bickley and Ewen, eds., *Memphis Tennessee Garrison*, 100.

35. Tadlock, "Coal Camps and Character," 22.

36. C. F. Biggert to F. B. Dunbar, June 14, 26, 1918.

37. Interview with Anlis Lee.

38. Interview with Woolford Griffey.

39. Laing, "The Negro Miner," 75.

40. "Benham, Wisconsin Steel Co.," 4.

41. Interview with Della Watts; interview with Gean Austin; interview with Eddie McDonald; interview with Sadie Long.

42. Maggard, "From Farm to Coal Camp," 16–17.

43. Bickley and Ewen, eds., *Memphis Tennessee Garrison*, 98.

44. Greene, "Strategies for Survival," 37–39.

45. Interview with Dorothy Morrow.

46. Maggard, "From Farm to Coal Camp," 17.

47. Trotter, "Black Miners," 275–77.

48. Bickley and Ewen, eds., *Memphis Tennessee Garrison*, 96.

49. "Fourth of July Celebration" (poster and program).

Chapter 3: "I Don't Know Where To, but We're Moving"

1. The Battle of Blair Mountain, the Ludlow Massacre, the West Virginia Mine Wars, to name a few coalfield conflicts. Corbin, *Life, Work, and Rebellion;* Corbin, "Class over Caste." The quotation in the title appears in the Afterword.

2. Kelly, *Race, Class, and Power.*

3. George A. Ranney to F. J. O'Connel, May 26, 1922.

4. Laing, "The Negro Miner," 76–77.

5. Interview with Willie Watts Jr.

6. Eller, *Miners, Millhands, and Mountaineers*, 171–72.

7. Bickley and Ewen, eds., *Memphis Tennessee Garrison*, 93.

8. Interview with Woolford Griffey.

9. LaLone, "Recollections about Life," 97.

10. Portelli, "Patterns of Paternalism," 145.

11. Ibid., 144–45.

12. See Bailey, "A Judicious Mixture"; Lewis, *Black Coal Miners;* Kelly, *Race, Class, and Power.*

13. Shifflett, "What Were Coal Towns Really Like?" 22–23.

14. Interview with Andrea D. Massey; interview with Eddie McDonald.

15. Trotter, "Black Miners," 287.

16. Turner and Cabbell, "Introduction," 16–18; Lewis, *Black Coal Miners*, 81.

17. Henever, *Which Side Are You On?* 43–44, 60.

18. United Mine Workers of America, "African-Americans."

19. Quoted in Lewis, *Black Coal Miners*, 304.

20. Interview with Gean Austin.

21. Lewis, *Black Coal Miners*, 306.

22. Interview with William Bosch.

23. Trotter "Black Miners," 281–82.

24. Lewis, *Black Coal Miners*, 305.

25. Hayden, "Blacks," 129; see also Cabbell, "Black Invisibility"; and Wright, "Black Appalachian Invisibility."

26. Hayden, "Blacks," 129.

27. Bickley and Ewen, eds., *Memphis Tennessee Garrison*, 112.

28. Greene, "Strategies For Survival," 43.

29. Trotter, "Black Miners," 295. Bickley and Ewen, eds., *Memphis Tennessee Garrison*, 158–84, also discuss this point.

30. Allen, "Blacks in Appalachia," 50; see also Sullivan, *Coal Men and Coal Towns*, 187.

31. Lewis, *Black Coal Miners*, 143.

32. Trotter, "Black Miners," 277.

33. Ibid., 281.

34. Interview with Gean Austin.

35. Henever, *Which Side Are You On?* 181–82.

36. Lewis, *Black Coal Miners*, 180; interview with William H. Turner; interview with Woolford Griffey.

37. Turner, "Appalachians, Black," 141. Black Appalachian migration streams continue unabated. Appalachia as a whole had a net loss of 6,444 African American residents between 1975 and 1980 due to migration, and about two-thirds of that loss occurred in southern Appalachia. Out migration from central Appalachia composed the other third. Between 1985 and 1990 some two hundred thousand black migrants had taken up residence in the region, and another 180,000 had moved away from the region. This net gain of about twenty thousand African American migrants occurred predominantly in the South, reversing by a wide margin the losses of the 1970s. By 1990, northern Appalachia had a net gain in black residents from migration, while the central portion of the region had a small net loss of about the same size it had in 1980. Obermiller and Howe, "New Paths and Patterns,"; Smith and Pederson, "South Toward Home,"; and, Frey, "Migration to the South."

38. Interview with Eddie McDonald.

39. Philliber and Obermiller, "Black Appalachian Migrants," 115; see also Hill, "Black Home"; and Burdette, "A School's Success Story."

Chapter 4: "Sing a Song of 'Welfare'"

1. The quotation in the chapter title is taken from the title of a song, "Sing a Song of 'Welfare'" (Crawford, *Building the Workingman's Paradise*, 55–57). Hays, *A History of Cumberland*, 7.

2. Banks, "Coal Miners and Firebrick Workers," 92–93.

3. "Benham, Wisconsin Steel Co.," 3.

4. Eller, *Miners, Millhands, and Mountaineers*, 190–91.

5. Crawford, *Building the Workingman's Paradise*; Levy, *Contemporary Urban Planning*.

6. Another noteworthy use of existing planning methods to build a company town was attempted by George McMurty, president of a steel mill near Pittsburgh. In the mid-1890s, McMurty hired the famous Boston landscape firm of Frederick Law Olmstead, Sr. to design the town of Vandergrift, Penn-

sylvania to house his employees. A central green, paved streets, running water, sewer systems, and electricity were put in place, but in contrast to traditional company towns, employees purchased their own lots and arranged construction of their houses. Low cost loans were provided through a company-financed savings and loan bank. McMurty's company town provided homes primarily for higher-paid and "loyal" workers who had helped to defeat a unionization drive. Two other nearby developments provided housing opportunities for lower-paid workers. A fence was erected later to separate McMurty's development from the other two areas. Fannie Mae Foundation, "Before EAH," 7.

7. Tone, *The Business of Benevolence*, 74.

8. International Harvester, "Harvester Town," 3.

9. Crawford, *Building the Workingman's Paradise*, 43; see also Portelli, "Patterns of Paternalism."

10. Portelli, "Patterns of Paternalism," 142.

11. Kelemen, "A History of Lynch," 175.

12. Tone, *The Business of Benevolence*, 23.

13. Ibid., 21. For more extensive discussions of welfare capitalism, see also Brandes, *American Welfare Capitalism;* Brody, *Workers in Industrial America;* Dore, *Stock Market Capitalism;* Hennen, *The Americanization of West Virginia;* and, Jacoby, *Modern Manors.*

14. Quoted in Tone, *The Business of Benevolence*, 37.

15. Ibid., 39.

16. Ibid., 50–51.

17. Ibid., 71.

18. Ibid., 22.

19. Jacoby, *Modern Manors*, 13–20.

20. Interview with William Bosch.

21. Crawford, *Building the Workingman's Paradise*, 55.

22. Ibid., 56–57.

23. Munn, "The Development of Model Towns," 247.

24. Ibid., 248–49.

25. Ibid., 251; see also Campbell, "Coal Towns," 53.

26. Tadlock, "Coal Camps and Character," 22.

27. Quoted in Munn, "The Development of Model Towns," 253.

28. Lewis, "Coal Miners and the Social Equality Wedge," 300.

29. "Benham, Wisconsin Steel Co.," 4.

30. H. F. Perkins to W. A. Tucker, Jan. 25, 1913.

31. H. F. Perkins to W. A. Tucker, March 28, Aug. 23, 1913.

32. W. A. Tucker to H. F. Perkins, Jan. 1, 1914.

33. Trotter, "Black Miners," 292–93.

34. H. F. Perkins to W. A. Tucker, March 28,1913.

35. Crawford, *Building the Workingman's Paradise*, 204–5.

Chapter 5: "Living Tolerably Well Together"

1. The quotation in the chapter title, from an interview with William Turner, is his description of living in Lynch. There is an extensive photographic record of the two towns. Both companies hired industrial photographers to send photographs to company headquarters in Chicago and Pittsburgh on a bi-weekly basis. Initially, these photographs were meant to document industrial development; thus, they show machinery and buildings rather than people. Later, however, both companies photographed the work and life of the communities to illustrate stories in company magazines.

2. Hale, "Wisconsin Steel Co.," 24.

3. Schertz, *Harlan County Coal Camps*, 1; "Benham, Wisconsin Steel Co."

4. Wilson, "Soil Conservation?" 15.

5. Wilson, "Mountain Legend"; Winston, "The Story of Benham."

6. Johnson, "A History of Lynch District," 2; Kentucky Coal Council, "Coal Education."

7. Bickley and Ewen, eds., *Memphis Tennessee Garrison*, 116.

8. Johnson, "A History of Lynch District," 2–5; see also Kelemen, "A History of Lynch."

9. Risden, "Some of Cumberland's 150–Year History," 1; Hays, "A History of Cumberland," 1; City of Cumberland, *Facts of Cumberland, Kentucky.*

10. McDougal, "New Landlords," 2.

11. Ibid.; Kelemen, "A History of Lynch," 157.

12. International Harvester, "Harvest of Happiness," 15–16.

13. International Harvester, "Harvester Town," 3.

14. Interview with William Bosch.

15. Interview with Dorothy Morrow; interview with Johnnie Jones; McDougal, "New Landlords," 2; Kelemen, "A History of Lynch," 161.

16. Johnson, "A History of Lynch District," 2, quoted in Kelemen, "A History of Lynch," 160. Italian stone masons were the one major exception to using ethnic workers only as miners. The highly skilled Italians were responsible for building most of Lynch's major public buildings and offices as well as other stone structures in the community.

17. Hill, "Black Home in Appalachia," 10.

18. Johnson, "A History of Lynch District," 6.

19. Hill, "Black Home in Appalachia," 10.

20. Johnson, "A History of Lynch District," 12, 14.

21. Both the Union of Lynch Employees and the Benham Employees Association were later chartered as locals by the Progressive Mine Workers of America, a United Mine Workers of America rival in Harlan County. The Lynch local of the Progressive Mine Workers of America later dissolved itself and affiliated with the United Mine Workers of America in October of 1937.

22. Hevener, *Which Side Are You On?* 113–14.

23. Johnson, "A History of Lynch District," 11, 13–14.

24. Interview with Woolford Griffey; interview with Alfonso Simms; Hill, "Black Home in Appalachia," 11–12.

25. Johnson, "A History of Lynch District," 17–18; interview with Woolford Griffey; interview with Eddie McDonald.

26. Interview with William Bosch.

27. Kelemen, "A History of Lynch," 165, 175.

28. International Harvester, "Harvest of Happiness," 15–16; Black Diamond Web-site at <http://home.earthlink.net/~bela1>.

29. Johnson, "A History of Lynch District," 12.

30. Interview with Dorothy Morrow.

31. Interview with Woolford Griffey; *Sojourner* (1980): 8.

32. International Harvester press release; "Benham, Wisconsin Steel Co."

33. Johnson, "A History of Lynch District," 7; Kelemen, "A History of Lynch," 168–69. The major criticism by one Lynch teacher was the "lack of manual work to interest deficient students."

34. Interview with Della Watts; interview with Eddie McDonald; *Sojourner* (1980): 8.

35. International Harvester, "School Notes and Quotes," 18.

36. Interview with Andrea D. Massey; interview with Gean Austin; interview with William H. Turner.

37. Interview with William Bosch; Johnson, "A History of Lynch District," 7, 8.

38. Benham Amusement Association (mimeo); Johnson, "A History of Lynch District," 6.

39. Interview with Gean Austin.

40. International Harvester, "Quintet Tours South," 18.

41. Interview with Willie Watts Jr.; William Bosch to Thomas Wagner, May 31, 2003; Black Diamond Web-site at <http://home.earthlink.net/~bela1>.

42. Interview with Woolford Griffey; interview with William Bosch; Black Diamond Web-site at <http://home.earthlink.net/~bela1>; Kelemen, "A History of Lynch," 67–68.

Chapter 6: "What Kept You Standing, Why Didn't You Fall?"

1. The quotation in the chapter title is from the title of a sermon described by William H. Turner in the Afterword. It is a paraphrase of a statement by Joe Louis. Eller, *Miners, Millhands, and Mountaineers;* Corbin, *Life, Work, and Rebellion,* quoted in Munn, "The Development of Model Towns," 243; see also Sullivan, *Coal Men and Coal Towns.*

2. Shifflett, *Coal Towns;* LaLone, "Recollections about Life"; Fishback, "The Miner's Work Environment."

3. Shifflett, *Coal Towns,* 23; Lewis, "Introduction," 17.

4. Interview with Gean Austin.

5. Hurst, "Weekend in Benham," 2.

6. Interview with Della Watts; *Sojourner* (1980): 8; interview with William H. Turner.

7. Interview with Gean Austin.

8. Interview with William Bosch.

9. Interview with Eddie McDonald.

10. Unsigned correspondence, March 23, July 20, 1920.

11. *Sojourner* (1981): 8; interview with Gean Austin; interview with Andrea D. Massey.

12. Interview with Della Watts; interview with Gean Austin.

13. Interview with Eddie McDonald.

14. Interview with William Bosch.

15. H. F. Perkins to W. C. Tucker, Jan. 25, 1913. In a subsequent letter to Tucker, dated March 18, 1913, Perkins reluctantly approved constructing the building because Cyrus McCormick, owner of International Harvester, "had given his word and it must be carried out." C. F. Biggert to S. B. White, Dec. 1, 1922; H. F. Perkins to W. A. Tucker, Aug. 23, 1913, Jan. 1, 1914.

16. Interview with William Bosch.

17. Interview with Woolford Griffey; Hill, "Black Home, 11; interview with Gean Austin; Tompkins, "Benham's Black Miners."

18. Interview with William Bosch; Richardson, "Growing Up in Lynch," 12–15.

Chapter 7: "One Close Community"

1. Interview with Fred Lickerman by Roger Guy, Chicago, April 4, 1994, in Guy, "Diversity to Unity"; interview with Ralph Bowles. The quotation in the chapter title is from an interview with Gean Austin and is his description of living in Lynch.

2. Wagner and Obermiller, "Going Home without the Trip," 216–17; see also Johnson, "Out of Appalachia."

3. Wagner and Obermiller, "Going Home without the Trip," 221–24.

4. Ibid., 220–21.

5. Obermiller and Wagner, "Cincinnati's 'Second Minority,'" 193.

6. Obermiller and Wagner, "'Hands-across-the-Ohio,'" 121.

7. Frazier, *Black Bourgeoisie,* 204.

8. Phillips, *Alabama North.* This pattern of social life is reflected in the Eastern Kentucky Social Club.

9. Jaffe, "Chicago Club Helps Blacks," 1.

10. Interview with Eddie McDonald; interview with Porter G. Peeples Jr.

11. Interview with Willie Watts Jr.; interview with Della Watts.

12. Interview with Willie Watts Jr.

13. Ibid.; interview with Gean Austin. In just a few short years the Eastern Kentucky Social Club evolved into a national organization, with a meeting of chapter presidents in April of each year to review plans for the annual Labor Day reunion and schedule the site of future reunions. Current members are informed about events through newsletters, chapter meetings, and the club's Web-site at <http://www.eksc-ca.com>, hosted by the California chapter.

14. Interview with Willie Watts Jr.; Eastern Kentucky Social Club Web-site at <http://www.eksc-ca.com>.

15. Interview with Willie Watts Jr. The Rosenwald Harlanites is a another African American organization founded by current and former residents of Harlan County, Kentucky. The group is composed of graduates of Rosenwald High School, an all-black public school established in 1920 by Chicago philanthropist Julius Rosenwald. The first meeting of the Harlanite Club was held in Detroit in 1969, and the group organized as a national association in 1976. Biennial reunions are held for the purpose of raising funds for college scholarships. The 2002 reunion was held in Chicago. The Web-site is at <http://www.rosenwaldharlanites.org>.

16. Interview with Willie Watts Jr.; interview with Della Watts; interview with Andrea D. Massey.

17. Interview with Della Watts.

18. Interview with Eddie McDonald.

19. Davis, "Heritage of Black Miners."

20. Heider, "Miners' Families Gather," 1B.

21. Interview with Andrea D. Massey.

22. Mead, "Memories Draw Generations Back," C1, C2; interview with Porter G. Peeples.

23. Eastern Kentucky Social Club Web-site at <http://www.eksc-ca.com>; Massey, "Eastern Kentucky Social Club Biography."

24. Interview with Della Watts; interview with Gene Austin.

25. Bickley and Ewen, eds., *Memphis Tennessee Garrison*, 81.

Chapter 8: "They Love Coming Home"

1. The quotation in the chapter title is from an interview with Andrea Massey, who discussed the Memorial Day activities hosted by the Lynch chapter of the EKSC.

2. Trotter, *River Jordan*, 21.

3. Wagner and Obermiller, "Going Home without the Trip," 215.

4. Hevener, *Which Side Are You On?* Scott, *Two Sides to Everything;* Jones, *Growing Up Hard;* Freese, *Coal.*

5. Greene, "Strategies for Survival"; Munn, "The Development of Model Towns."

6. Munn, "The Development of Model Towns," 246.

7. Bickley and Ewen, eds., *Memphis Tennessee Garrison*, 121.

8. Interview with Andrea D. Massey.

Afterword

1. "What Holds You Up?" is the title of a sermon I heard at the First Baptist Church in Lynch, Kentucky, preached by the Rev. J. C. Middlebrooks in, as best I remember, 1958. He used the metaphor the way black Baptist preachers often use parables. In the end—the moral of the story—he told people that it was God who held them up. I took the liberty of invoking his usage of the black southern dialect that was so common among the black coal miners I knew in my youth— call it the official ebonics of that day—and popularized in the works of Paul Lawrence Dunbar. All other references to Joe Louis, named Joseph Louis Barrow at birth, appear in Schwartz, "'Brown Bomber' Was a Hero to All."

2. Hughes, from the poem "Mother to Son," in *Collected Poems*, ed. Rampersad and Roessel; Cabbell, "Black Invisibility and Racism in Appalachia." Cabbell's master's thesis, "References and Resources on Black Appalachians," provides the most comprehensive bibliography on the subject. When asked if blacks in Appalachia identify themselves as Appalachian, Alex Haley responded, "No, they don't because that is superseded, if not drowned, in being black. Probably the most Appalachian man I've met is Bill Turner, a professor at Berea College. Bill is a scholar on blacks in Appalachia but I've never heard Bill refer to himself as an Appalachian. I think the most you would get from any of these people is that they would say they are blacks in Appalachia, . . . If you deal with

being black, you really don't have the time to deal with being Appalachian."
Hawthorne, "Alex Haley at Home in East Tennessee," 39–40.

3. Klotter, "The Black South and White Appalachia"; see also Lewis, *Black Coal Miners*.

4. Corbin, "Class over Caste," 93.

5. Author's personal files. Obituary documents were donated by two funeral homes, long since out of business in the county. Mitchell Funeral Home, the only black funeral business in Harlan County, did business for more than thirty years [between 1935 and 1970]. After legal segregation ended in the mid-1960s, Mitchell's went out of business, and the white undertaker, Johnson's Funeral Home, began service to blacks.

6. In *Appalachian Values*, Loyal Jones lists religion first among the values important in Appalachian life and culture, followed, in order, by independence, self-reliance and pride, neighborliness, familism, personalism, humility and modesty, love of place, patriotism, sense of beauty, and a sense of humor.

Bibliography

Abbreviations

AA Photos and interviews in the Appalachian Archive, Southeast Kentucky Community College, Cumberland.
AF Tapes and documents in the authors' files in Cincinnati.
CL Documents in the Cumberland City Files, Rebecca Caudill Public Library, Cumberland, Ky.
SE Documents in the Benham and Lynch Collection, Appalachian Archive, Southeast Kentucky Community College, Cumberland.
UK Documents in the Special Collection, Margaret King Library, University of Kentucky, Lexington.
WI Documents in the State Historical Society of Wisconsin, Madison.

Interviews

Austin, Gean. Lynch, Ky., July 23, 1997. AF.
Bowles, Ralph. Cleveland, Ohio, July 14, 1997. AF.
Bosch, Audra. Cincinnati, Ohio, Nov. 8, 2000. AF.
Bosch, William. Cincinnati, Ohio, Nov. 8, 2000. AF.
Griffey, Woolford. Benham, Ky., May 1979. Interview by Jeff Turner. AA.
Hannah, James. Harlan County, Ky., Feb. 13, 1980. Interview by Linda Parker. AA
Jones, Johnnie. Lynch, Ky., Sept. 22, 1988. Interview by Tonya Pettygrue. AA.
Lee, Anlis. Lynch, Ky., Feb. 14, 1980. Interview by Debbie Lee. AA
Long, Sadie. Lynch, Ky., Feb. 1, 1985. Interview by Cynthia Tinsley. AA.
McDonald, Alberta. Detroit, Mich., July 15, 1997. AF.
McDonald, Eddie. Detroit, Mich., July 15, 1997. AF.
Morrow, Dorothy. Benham, Ky., Nov. 13, 1989. Interview by Tim Bullock. AA.
Massey, Andrea D., Lynch, Ky., July 23, 1997. AF.
Peeples, Porter G., Jr. Lexington, Ky., June 9, 1997. AF.
Simms, Alfonso. Lynch, Ky., March 25, 1980. Interview by Debbie Lee. AA.
Turner, William H. Lexington, Ky., April 24, 1997. AF.

Watts, Della. Cleveland, Ohio, July 13, 1997. AF.
Watts, Willie, Jr. Cleveland, Ohio, July 13, 1997. AF.

Correspondence and Other Documents

Benham Amusement Association, undated mimeo, box 9, SE.
B. W. Batchelder to R. A. Walter, May 24, 1921, box 11, SE.
C. F. Biggert to Alexander Legge, May 23, 1923, box 9, SE.
C. F. Biggert to F. B. Dunbar, June 14, 1918, box 25, SE.
C. F. Biggert to F. B. Dunbar, June 26, 1918, box 25, SE.
C. F. Biggert to S. B. White, Dec. 1, 1922, box 9, SE.
F. B. Dunbar to C. F. Biggert, June 26, 1920, box 6, SE.
"Fourth of July Celebration," 1927 (poster and typescript program schedules), box 2, SE.
George A. Ranney to F. J. O'Connel, May 26, 1922, box 11, SE.
H. F. Perkins to W. A. Tucker, Jan. 25, 1913, box 5, SE.
H. F. Perkins to W. A. Tucker, March 28, 1913, box 5, SE.
H. F. Perkins to W. A. Tucker, Aug. 23, 1913, box 5, SE.
International Harvester press release, undated, box 2, SE.
R. A. Walter to B. W. Batchelder, April 19, 1920, box 11, SE.
R. A. Walter to B. W. Batchelder, March 8, 1921, box 11, SE.
Unsigned carbon copy of correspondence, March 23, July 20, 1920, box 6, SE.
W. A. Tucker to H. F. Perkins, Jan. 1, 1914, box 5, SE.
William Bosch to Thomas Wagner, May 2003, AF.

Other Sources

Alexander, J. Trent. "Great Migrations: Race and Community in the Southern Exodus, 1917–1970." Ph.D. diss., Carnegie-Mellon University, 2001.
Allen, Fayetta A. "Blacks in Appalachia." *Black Scholar* 5, no. 9 (1974): 42–51.
Armistead, Robert, with S. L. Gardner. *Black Days, Black Dust: Memories of an African-American Coal Miner.* Knoxville: University of Tennessee Press, 2002.
Associated Press. "Trying to Keep a Culture Alive." *Cleveland Plain Dealer,* April 4, 1993, 15B.
Bailey, Kenneth R. "A Judicious Mixture: Negroes and Immigrants in the West Virginia Mines, 1880–1917." In *Blacks in Appalachia,* ed. William H. Turner and Edward J. Cabbell, 117–32. Lexington: University Press of Kentucky, 1985.
Banks, Alan. "Coal Miners and Firebrick Workers: The Structure of Work Relations in Two Eastern Kentucky Communities." *Appalachian Journal* 11, nos. 1 and 2 (1983–84): 85–102.

Bates, Beth Tompkins. *Pullman Porters and the Rise of Protest Politics in Black America, 1925–1945.* Chapel Hill: University of North Carolina Press. 2001.

"Benham, Wisconsin Steel Co. Operation, Model Community." *Harlan Daily Enterprise,* n.d., box 2, SE.

Bennett, Lerone, Jr. *The Shaping of Black America.* Chicago: Johnson Publishing, 1975.

Bickley, Ancella R., and Lynda Ann Ewen, eds. *Memphis Tennessee Garrison: The Remarkable Story of a Black Appalachian Woman.* Athens: Ohio University Press, 2001.

"Black Appalachians." *Mountain Life and Work* 58, no. 9 (1982), special issue.

"Black Appalachians." *Mountain Life and Work* 64, no. 2 (1988), special issue.

"Black Appalachians in the City." *Mountain Life and Work* 52, no. 8 (1976): 18–19.

Black Diamond. Web-site at <http://home.earthlink.net/~bela1> accessed on Sept. 14, 2000.

Brandes, Stuart D. *American Welfare Capitalism, 1880–1940.* Chicago: University of Chicago Press, 1976.

Brody, David. *Workers in Industrial America: Essays on the Twentieth Century Struggle.* 2d ed. New York: Oxford University Press, 1993.

Brown, James S., and George A. Hillery. "The Great Migration, 1940–1960." In *The Southern Appalachian Region: A Survey,* ed. Thomas R. Ford, 53–78. Lexington: University Press of Kentucky, 1962.

Burdette, Dick. "A School's Success Story." *Lexington Herald-Leader,* July 23, 1997, B1, B3.

Cabbell, Edward J. "Black Diamonds: The Search for Blacks in Appalachian Literature and Writing." *Now and Then* 3, no. 1 (1986): 11–13.

———. "Black Invisibility and Racism in Appalachia: An Informal Survey." *Appalachian Journal* 8, no. 1 (1980): 48–54.

———. "History Uncovers the Role of Black Appalachian Women." *Now and Then* 3, no. 1 (1986): 13–15.

———. "References and Resources on Black Appalachians." Master's thesis. Appalachian State University, Boone, N.C., 1982

Campbell, Shirley Bell. "Coal Towns." *Goldenseal* 13, no. 2 (1987): 53.

"Christmas." *Sojourner* 1, no. 2 (1980): 5. UK.

City of Cumberland. n.d. *Facts of Cumberland, Kentucky.* CL.

"Coal Miners Wanted: In Southeastern Kentucky, They See a Rise in Demand." *Wall Street Journal,* March 6, 2001, 1.

Corbin, David A. "Class over Caste: Interracial Solidarity in a Company Town."

In *Blacks in Appalachia,* ed. William H. Turner and Edward J. Cabbell, 93–113. Lexington: University Press of Kentucky, 1985.

———. *Life, Work, and Rebelion in the Coal Fields: The Southern West Virginia Miners, 1880–1922.* Urbana: University of Illinois Press, 1981.

Crawford, Margaret. *Building the Workingman's Paradise: The Design of American Company Towns.* New York: Verso, 1995.

Davis, Merlene. "Heritage of Black Miners Is in Danger." *Lexington Herald-Leader,* Sept. 10, 2000, J1. Web-site at <http://www.kentuckyconnect.com/heraldleader/news/091000/kylifedocs/merle10.htm> accessed on Sept. 11, 2000.

———. "Jealousy Not Invited to Annual Reunion." *Lexington Herald-Leader,* Sept. 10, 1992, 4.

Deskins, David, and Jennifer Kovach. *The Collected Works of Effie Waller Smith.* New York: Oxford University Press, 1991.

Dore, Ronald. *Stock Market Capitalism: Welfare Capitalism.* New York: Oxford University Press, 2000.

Dunaway, Wilma. *Slavery in the American South.* New York: Cambridge University Press, 2003.

Eastern Kentucky Social Club. "Program for Twenty-eighth Annual Reunion" (mimeo, 1997). AF.

———. Web-site at <http://www.eksc-ca.com> accessed on June 11, 2003.

Eller, Ronald D. *Miners, Millhands, and Mountaineers: Industrialization of the Appalachian South, 1880–1930.* Knoxville: University of Tennessee Press, 1982.

Elliott, Brook. "Coalfield of Dreams." *Home and Away,* May 2000, 18–19.

Fannie Mae Foundation. "Before EAH: The Company Town." *House Facts and Findings* 2 (Summer 2000): 7.

Fishback, Price V. "The Miner's Work Environment: Safety and Company Towns in the Early 1900s." In *The United Mine Workers of America: A Model of Industrial Solidarity?* ed. John H. M. Laslett, 201–23. University Park: Pennsylvania State University Press, 1996.

Frazier, E. Franklin. *Black Bourgeoisie.* New York: Free Press, 1957.

Freese, Barbara. *Coal: A Human History.* Cambridge, Mass.: Perseus Publishing, 2003.

Frey, William H. "Migration to the South Brings U.S. Blacks Full Circle." *Population Today* 29, no. 4 (2001): 1, 4.

Goode, James B. "Coal Company Schools." In *The Encyclopedia of Appalachia,* ed. Rudy Abramson and Jean Haskell Speer. Knoxville: University of Tennessee Press, in press.

———. n.d. "Introduction to Coal Camp Database." Web-site at <http://

www.coaleducation.org/coalhistory/coaltowns/introduction_to_coal_camp.htm> accessed on June 11, 2003.

Greene, Janet W. "Strategies for Survival: Women's Work in the Southern West Virginia Coalfields." *West Virginia History* 49 (1990): 37–54.

Guillebeaux, Jack. "Not Just Whites in Appalachia." In *Blacks in Appalachia*, ed. William H. Turner and Edward J. Cabbell, 207–10. Lexington: University Press of Kentucky, 1985.

Guy, Roger. "Diversity to Unity: Uptown's Southern Migrants, 1950–1970." Ph.D. diss., University of Wisconsin-Milwaukee, 1996.

Hale, Sam. "The Wisconsin Steel Company." *Harvester World*, Nov. 24, 1909. WI.

Hawkins, Homer C. "Trends in Black Migration from 1863 to 1960." *Phylon* 34, no. 2 (1973): 140–52.

Hawthorne, Ann. "Alex Haley at Home in East Tennessee." *Appalachia: Journal of the Appalachian Regional Commission* 25, no. 1 (1992): 33–40.

Hayden, Wilburn, Jr. "Blacks: An Invisible Institution in Appalachia?" In *The Impact of Institutions in Appalachia: Proceedings of the Eighth Annual Appalachian Studies Conference*, ed. Jim Lloyd and Anne C. Campbell, 128–47. Boone, N.C.: Appalachian Consortium Press, 1986.

Hays, Patsy Anne. "A History of Cumberland, Kentucky from 1870 to 1941." Typescript, n.d. CL.

Heider, Timothy. "Miners' Families Gather for Reunion." *Cleveland Plain Dealer*, Sept. 5, 1994, 1B.

Hennen, John C. *The Americanization of West Virginia: Creating a Modern Industrial State, 1916–1925*. Lexington: University Press of Kentucky, 1996.

Hevener, John W. *Which Side Are You On? The Harlan County Coal Miners, 1931–39*. Urbana: University of Illinois Press, 1978 (2002).

Hickam, Homer. *Sky of Stone*. New York: Delacorte Press, 2001.

Hill, Bob. "Black Home in Appalachia." *Courier-Journal Magazine* (Louisville), June 28, 1987, 6–12.

Hurst, Mercedes J. "Weekend in Benham: A Portrait of a Kentucky Mining Town Where Harvester People Work and Play and Worship." *Harvester World*, Dec. 1951, 2 (mimeo). SE.

Inscoe, John C. "Mountain Masters: Slaveholding in Western North Carolina." *North Carolina Historical Review* 61, no. 2 (1984): 143–73.

———. "Race and Racism in Nineteenth-Century Southern Appalachia: Myths, Realities, and Ambiguities." In *Appalachia in the Making: The Mountain South in the Nineteenth Century*, ed. Mary Beth Pudup, Dwight B. Billings, and Altina L. Waller, 103–31. Chapel Hill: University of North Carolina Press, 1995.

————, ed. *The Mountain South from Slavery to Segregation.* Lexington: University Press of Kentucky, 2001.

International Harvester. "Benham Works, Children Shout." *Coal Mines: Benham* 2, no. 5 (1945): 5, 7. SE.

————. "Coal Miner." *International Harvester Today* 1, no. 7 (1950): 19–23. SE.

————. "Harvester Town: Black Diamonds from Kentucky Hills Go into IH Steel." *Coal Mines: Benham* 3, no. 7 (1946): 2–3. SE.

————. "Harvest of Happiness." *Coal Mines: Benham* 5, no. 3 (1948): 15–16. SE.

————. "Quintet Tours South." *Coal Mines: Benham* 1, no. 10 (1944): 10, 18. SE.

————. "School Notes and Quotes." *Coal Mines: Benham* 2, no. 5 (1945): 18. SE.

Jacoby, Sanford M. *Modern Manors: Welfare Capitalism since the New Deal.* Princeton: Princeton University Press, 1997.

Jaffe, Greg. "Chicago Club Helps Blacks Find Pride in Segregated Past." *Wall Street Journal,* March 12, 1997, 1.

Johnson, Susan Allyn. "Out of Appalachia: Southern White Migration to Akron, Ohio, 1900–1960." Ph.D. diss., Ohio State University, 2002.

Johnson, T. E. "A History of Lynch District: 1917–1957" (mimeo, nd.d.). United States Steel Corp., Lynch, Ky. SE.

Jones, G. C. *Growing Up Hard in Harlan County.* Lexington: University Press of Kentucky, 1985.

Jones, Loyal. *Appalachian Values.* Ashland, Ky.: Jessie Stewart Foundation, 1994

Kelemen, Thomas A. "A History of Lynch, Kentucky, 1917–1930." *Filson Club History Quarterly* 48, no. 2 (1974): 156–76.

Kelly, Brian. *Race, Class, and Power in the Alabama Coalfields, 1908–1921.* Urbana: University of Illinois Press, 2001.

Kentucky Coal Council. Web-site at <http://www.coaleducation.org> accessed on Oct. 16, 2001.

Kleber, John E., ed. *The Kentucky Encyclopedia.* Lexington: University Press of Kentucky. 1992.

Klotter, James C. "The Black South and White Appalachia." *Journal of American History* 66, no. 4 (1980): 832–49.

Laing, James T. "The Negro Miner in West Virginia." In *Blacks in Appalachia,* ed. William H. Turner and Edward J. Cabbell, 71–79. Lexington: University Press of Kentucky, 1985.

LaLone, Mary B. "Recollections about Life in Appalachia's Coal Camps: Positive or Negative?" *Journal of the Appalachian Studies Association* 7 (1995): 91–100.

Laslett, John H. M., ed. *The United Mine Workers of America: A Model of Industrial Solidarity?* University Park: Pennsylvania State University Press, 1996.

Lee, Lloyd G. *A Brief History of Kentucky and Its Counties.* Berea: Kentucky Imprints, 1981.

Levy, John M. *Contemporary Urban Planning.* Upper Saddle River: Prentice-Hall, 2000.

Lewis, Helen. "Introduction." In Builder Levy, *Images of Appalachian Coalfields.* Philadelphia: Temple University Press, 1989.

Lewis, Ronald L. "African-American Convicts in the Coal Mines of Southern Appalachia." In *The Mountain South from Slavery to Segregation,* ed. John C. Inscoe, 259–83. Lexington: University Press of Kentucky, 2001.

———. *Black Coal Miners in America: Race, Class, and Community Conflict, 1780–1980.* Lexington: University Press of Kentucky, 1987.

———. "Coal Miners and the Social Equality Wedge in Alabama, 1880–1908." In *The United Mine Workers of America: A Model of Industrial Solidarity?* ed. John H. M. Laslett, 297–319. University Park: Pennsylvania State University Press, 1996.

———. "From Peasant to Proletarian: The Migration of Southern Blacks to the Central Appalachian Coalfields." *Journal of Southern History* 55, no. 1 (1989): 77–101.

Maggard, Sally Ward. "From Farm to Coal Camp to Back Office and Mc-Donald's: Living in the Midst of Appalachia's Latest Transformation." *Journal of the Appalachian Studies Association* 6 (1994): 14–38.

Marsh, Betsa. "Pullman Built a Town to Last." *Cincinnati Enquirer,* Nov. 11, 2001, 3–5.

Massey, Andrea D. "Eastern Kentucky Social Club's Biography" (mimeo, 1997). AF.

McDougal, Angus. "New Landlords for Benham." *Harvester World,* Dec. 1960 (mimeo). WI.

McKinney, Gordon B. "Southern Mountain Republicans and the Negro, 1865–1900." *Journal of Southern History* 41, no. 4 (1975): 493–516.

Mead, Andy. "Memories Draw Generations Back to Lynch." *Lexington Herald-Leader,* May 27, 1991, C1, C2.

"Memorial Day." *Sojourner* 1, no. 3 (1981): 1–4. UK.

Morgan, Nicole. "A Way with Words: Affrilachian Poets Band Together for Inspiration, Mutual Support." *Lexington Herald-Leader,* Aug. 22, 2001, 9. Web-site at <http://www.kentuckyconnect.com/heraldleader/news/082201/communitydocs/22cover.htm> accessed on Aug. 24, 2001.

Munn, Robert F. "The Development of Model Towns in the Bituminous Coal Fields." *West Virginia History* 30, no. 3 (1979): 243–53.

Obermiller, Phillip J., and Steven R. Howe. "New Paths and Patterns of Appalachian Migration, 1975–1990." In *Appalachia: Social Context Past and Present*, ed. Phillip J. Obermiller and Michael E. Maloney, 89–97. 4th ed. Dubuque: Kendall/Hunt, 2002.

Obermiller, Phillip J., and Thomas E. Wagner. "Cincinnati's 'Second Minority': The Emergence of Appalachian Advocacy, 1953–1973." In *Appalachian Odyssey: Historical Perspectives on the Great Migration*, ed. Phillip J. Obermiller, Thomas E. Wagner, and E. Bruce Tucker, 193–214. Westport: Praeger Publishers, 2000.

———. "'Hands-across-the-Ohio': The Urban Initiatives of the Council of the Southern Mountains, 1954–1971." In *Appalachian Odyssey: Historical Perspectives on the Great Migration*, ed. Phillip J. Obermiller, Thomas E. Wagner, and E. Bruce Tucker, 121–40. Westport: Praeger Publishers, 2000.

Osborne, Theresa. "Coal Camp Life" (unpublished), 2002. Cumberland, Ky.: Appalachian Archives, Southeast Community College. AA.

Philliber, William W., and Phillip J. Obermiller. "Black Appalachian Migrants: The Issue of Dual Minority Status." In *Too Few Tomorrows: Urban Appalachians in the 1980s*, ed. Phillip J. Obermiller and William W. Philliber, 111–15. Boone, N.C.: Appalachian Consortium Press, 1987.

Phillips, Kimberley L. *Alabama North: African-American Migrants, Community, and Working-Class Activism in Cleveland*. Urbana: University of Illinois Press, 1999.

Portelli, Alessandro. "Patterns of Paternalism in Harlan County." *Appalachian Journal* 17, no. 2 (1990): 140–54.

———. "We Were Poor but . . . How Appalachians and Italians Look at Poverty." *Now and Then* 19 (2002): 31–35.

Pudup, Mary Beth. "Social Class and Economic Development in Southeast Kentucky, 1820–1880." In *Appalachian Frontiers: Settlement, Society and Development in the PreIndustrial Era*, ed. Robert D. Mitchell, 235–60. Lexington: University Press of Kentucky, 1991.

Rampersad, Arnold, and David Roessel, eds. *The Collected Poems of Langston Hughes*. New York: Alfred A. Knopf Publishers, 1994.

"Resident Population of Kentucky and Counties." *Kentucky State Data Center News* 19, no. 1 (200): 1–4.

Richardson, Jerry. "Growing Up in Lynch." *Appalachian Heritage* 24 (Summer 1996): 12–15.

Risden, Bill. "Some of Cumberland's 150–Year History Recalled." *Tri-City News* (Cumberland, Ky.), Sept. 10, 1986, 1.

Rosenwald Harlanites, Inc. "Building a Brighter Future" Web-site at <http:// www.rosenwaldharlanites.org> accessed on Jan. 16, 2003.

Salstrom, Paul. *Appalachia's Path to Dependency: Rethinking a Region's Economic History, 1730–1940.* Lexington: University Press of Kentucky, 1994.

Schertz, Ann E. *Harlan County Coal Camps: Lynch and Benham, Kentucky: Cultural Transition from Rural to Urban Communities: Industrial Documentary Photography, 1912–1948.* Cumberland, Ky.: Southeast Community College Appalachian Archives, 1987. SE.

Schwartz, Larry. "'Brown Bomber Was Hero to All.'" Web-site at <http:// msn.espn.go.com> accessed on June 12, 2003.

Scott, Shaunna. *Two Sides to Everything: The Cultural Construction of Class Consciousness in Harlan County, Kentucky.* Albany: State University of New York Press, 1995.

Scruggs, Afi-Odelia. "Coal Camps Full of Memories." *Cleveland Plain Dealer,* March 30, 2001, B1.

Shifflett, Crandall A. *Coal Towns: Life, Work, and Culture in Company Towns of Southern Appalachia, 1880–1960.* Knoxville: University of Tennessee Press, 1991.

———. "What Were Coal Towns Really Like?" *Appalachian Heritage* 20, no. 3 (1992): 21–24.

Smith, Vern E., and Daniel Pedersen. "South toward Home." *Newsweek,* July 14, 1997, 36, 38.

Sojourner. Vol. 1, no. 3 (1981), published cooperatively by the Eastern Kentucky Social Club and the Appalachian Center at the University of Kentucky. UK.

Stein, Herbert. "A Model of Philanthropy." *Wall Street Journal,* Feb. 24, 1998, A22.

Stuckert, Robert P. "Racial Violence in Southern Appalachia, 1880–1940." *Appalachian Heritage* 20, no. 2 (1992): 35–41.

Sullivan, Charles Kenneth. *Coal Men and Coal Towns: Development of the Smokeless Coalfields of Southern West Virginia, 1873–1923.* New York: Garland, 1989.

Sykes, Leonard, Jr., and Felicia Thomas-Lynn. "Graying NAACP Strives to Recruit Youth." *Cincinnati Enquirer,* Sept. 13, 2001, A3.

Tadlock, E. V. "Coal Camps and Character." *Mountain Life and Work* 4 (Jan. 1929): 20–23.

Taylor, Paul F. *Bloody Harlan: The United Mine Workers of America in Harlan County, Kentucky, 1931–1941.* New York: University Press of America, 1990.

Tehranian, Kathrine Kia. *Modernity, Space, and Power: The American City in Discourse and Practice.* Cresskill, N.J.: Hampton Press, 1995.

Tompkins, Wayne. "Benham's Black Miners Had Tough Time Moving Up: Harvester Mine Had No Black Boss until the 1970s." *Louisville Courier-Journal,* Dec. 22, 1999. Web-site at <http://www.courier-journal.com/localnews> accessed on Dec. 22, 1999.

Tone, Andrea. *The Business of Benevolence: Industrial Paternalism in Progressive America.* Ithaca: Cornell University Press, 1997.

Toyota Motor Manufacturing Kentucky. 2002. Web-site at <http://www.toyota georgetown.com> accessed on March 18, 2002.

Trotter, Joe William, Jr. "Black Miners in West Virginia: Class and Community Responses to Workplace Discrimination, 1920–1930." In *The United Mine Workers of America: A Model of Industrial Solidarity?* ed. John H. M. Laslett, 269–96. University Park: Pennsylvania State University Press, 1995.

———. *Coal, Class, and Color: Blacks in Southern West Virginia, 1915–32.* Urbana: University of Illinois Press, 1990.

———. "Race, Class, and Industrial Change: Black Migration to Southern West Virginia." In *The Great Migration in Historical Perspective: New Dimensions of Race, Class, and Gender,* ed. Joe William Trotter, Jr., 46–67. Bloomington: University of Indiana Press, 1991.

———. *River Jordan: African American Life in the Ohio River Valley.* Lexington: University Press of Kentucky, 1988.

Turner, William H. "Appalachians, Black." In *Encyclopedia of Southern Culture,* ed. Charles R. Wilson and William Ferris, 139–41. Chapel Hill: University of North Carolina Press, 1989.

———. "Between Berea (1904) and Birmingham (1908): The Rock and Hard Place for Blacks in Appalachia." In *Blacks in Appalachia,* ed. William H. Turner and Edward J. Cabbell, 11–19. Lexington: University Press of Kentucky, 1985.

———. "Essay on Black Mountain." E-mail to authors, 1999. AF.

———. "Introduction." In *Blacks in Appalachia,* ed. William H. Turner and Edward J. Cabbell, xvii–xxiii. Lexington: University Press of Kentucky, 1985.

United Mine Workers of America. "African-American Miners in the UMWA," 2001. Web-site at <http://www.umwa.org/history/race.shtml> accessed on Dec. 16, 2000.

Wagner, Thomas E., and Phillip J. Obermiller. "Going Home without the Trip: Appalachian Migrant Organizations." In *Appalachian Odyssey: Historical Perspectives on the Great Migration,* ed. Phillip J. Obermiller, Thomas E. Wagner, and E. Bruce Tucker, 215–30. Westport: Praeger Publishers, 2000.

Waller, Effie. *Rhymes from the Cumberland.* New York: Broadway Publishing, 1909.

Wilson, Grace. "Mountain Legend." *Coal Mines: Benham* 1, no. 4 (1944): 14.

Wilson, Mary Nell. "Soil Conservation?: This Coal Community Couldn't Do without It." *Harvester World* 45, no. 4 (1954): 15.

Winston, Amy. "The Story of Benham" (Benham, Ky.), n.d. Web-site at <http://www.uky.edu/~rsilver/benham.htm> accessed on Sept. 14, 2000.

Woodson, Carter G. "The Negroes of Cincinnati prior to the Civil War." *Journal of Negro History* 1, no. 1 (1916): 1–22.

Wright, Clarence. "Black Appalachian Invisibility—Myth or Reality?" *Black Appalachian Viewpoints* 1, no. 1 (1973): 1–3. UK.

Index

"aboveground railroad," 116, 117

African Americans: child labor, 34; as forced laborers, 10; invisibility, 45ff.; migration, 5, 7–11, 47–51, 102–4; in mining, 17ff.; NAACP, 46; population, 7–11, 49; in slavery, 5ff., 10; violence against, 6ff.; women, 33ff. *See also* race relations

Alexander, J. Trent, 8

Allen, Fayetta, 47

Appalachian Community Development Association (Cincinnati, Ohio), 101

Appalachian Festival (Cincinnati, Ohio), 101

Austin, Gean, 31, 43, 48, 83, 92, 93, 94, 96, 97, 105, 110

Baldwin, James, 122

Banks, Alan, 19, 52

Benham Amusement Association, 85

Benham Employees Association, 76

Benham, Ky., 5; founding, 2, 52–57, 68; Fourth of July celebration, 29, 34; map of, 3; schools, 30

Biggert, C.F., 15, 81

blacks. *See* African Americans

Black Mountain, 67, 68, 72, 93

"Bloody Harlan." *See* Harlan County

Bosch, William (Bill), 18, 44, 72, 78, 84, 90, 93, 96, 97, 98

Cannon, Jimmy, 129

Carter, George L., 114ff.

Charleston Club (Detroit, Mich.), 102

Cherokee. *See* Trail of Tears

Chicago Southern Center, 101

Chide, Elmer, 105

Chloe Creek (Cumberland Mountains), 1

churches: Benham Community Church, 16; Catholic Church of the Resurrection, 84; Community Church, 84; Goode Temple African Methodist Episcopal Church, 84; Mt. Sinai Baptist Church, 84; St. Nicholas Eastern Rite Orthodox, 84

Civil Rights Act of 1875, 1

Civil War, 6ff.

Coal Age journal, 63

coal camps, 11, 114–16

Coal: A Human History (Freese), 114

Coal Mines: Benham (International Harvester magazine), 72

coal towns: class structure, 41, 98; decline of, 47ff.; labor force, 40ff., 71–74; model, 4, 71, 109, 112, 114–16

Coalwood, W.V., 15, 114ff.

Commons, John. *See Review of Reviews*

company store, 24–27, 80ff.; scrip at, 26

company towns, 11–16; New England textile towns, 11–16. *See also* Benham, Ky.; Lynch, Ky.; Pullman, Ill.

Conn, Billy, 124

Consolidated Coal Company, 115

Corbin, David, 35, 91

Council of the Southern Mountains (Berea, Ky., and Chicago, Ill.), 101

Crawford, Margaret, 16, 63

Cumberland, Ky., 2, 70, 108; map of, 3

THOMAS E. WAGNER is university professor emeritus of planning and urban studies at the University of Cincinnati, where he also served as vice president for student affairs and services.

PHILLIP J. OBERMILLER is a center associate at the Appalachian Center at the University of Kentucky and a visiting professor of urban studies in the School of Planning at the University of Cincinnati.

WILLIAM H. TURNER is acting president of Kentucky State University, Frankfort. A college professor and administrator for most of his career, he was born in Lynch, Kentucky, and is a member of the Eastern Kentucky Social Club.

The University of Illinois Press
is a founding member of the
Association of American University Presses.

Composed in 10.5/13 Adobe Minion
at the University of Illinois Press
Designed by Dennis Roberts
Manufactured by Sheridan Books, Inc.

University of Illinois Press
1325 South Oak Street
Champaign, IL 61820-6903
www.press.uillinois.edu